Handbook of Catholic Social Teaching

Handbook of Catholic Social Teaching

A GUIDE FOR CHRISTIANS IN THE WORLD TODAY

Edited by Martin Schlag
Foreword by Peter K.A. Cardinal Turkson

THE CATHOLIC UNIVERSITY OF AMERICA PRESS

Washington, D.C.

Revised and translated from the original publication in Italian as *Economia e società: le sfide della responsabilità cristiana. Domande e risposte sul compendio della Dottrina sociale della Chiesa*, (Rome, Edusc, 2015). Italian copyright © 2015 EDUSC.

English translation copyright © 2017
The Catholic University of America Press
All rights reserved
The paper used in this publication meets the minimum requirements of American National Standards for Information Science—Permanence of Paper for Printed Library Materials, ANSI Z39.48–1984.
∞

Library of Congress Cataloging-in-Publication Data

Schlag, Martin, 1964–editor.
Handbook of Catholic social teaching : a guide for Christians in the world today / edited by Martin Schlag ; foreword by Peter Cardinal K.A.Turkson.
Economia e societá. English
 p. cm.
Washington, DC : Catholic University of America Press, 2017. |
 Includes bibliographical references and index.
LCCN 2016053096 | ISBN 9780813229324 (pbk. : alk. paper)
LCSH: Christian sociology—Catholic Church—Miscellanea.
LCC BX1753 .E2613 2017 | DDC 261.8088/282—dc23
LC record available at https://lccn.loc.gov/2016053096

Contents

Foreword

Peter K.A. Cardinal Turkson

"Whoever does not love a brother [or sister] whom he has seen, cannot love God whom he has not seen" (1 John 4:20). At the core of our faith are the two prescriptions of the Greatest Commandment (Matthew 22: 35–40 and Mark 12: 28–34) and they are indissolubly linked. Faith without charity is lifeless: "Faith of itself, if it does not have works, is dead" (James 2:17). And perhaps the strongest teaching Jesus ever gave remains the parable of the Good Samaritan (Luke 10:25–37).

We are inspired, we are moved, but what shall we do? How can we best respond?

Out of the faith experience of the ecclesial community flow the social repercussions of the Scriptures, of the gospel. Down through the ages, holy men and women, dioceses, ecclesial movements, and religious orders, inspired by faith and charity, have carried out every imaginable form of service to the poor and the needy, including prisoners and refugees, the sick and dying, pilgrims and slaves, and many more besides.

In this way, insisted St. John Paul II, "Christianity must be inserted in daily life and oriented to reforming the social reality. Human and Christian responsibility need to be exercised in these places: in family and in Church, in work and in politics."[1]

In the modern era, Pope Leo XIII was the first to formally articulate Catholic Social Teaching, which brings our faith and tradition to bear on the changing and challenging circumstances of modern society.

---

1 St. John Paul II, Homily at the Beatification of Adolph Kolping (1813–1865), October 27, 1991.

As a language of faith-in-action, of reflection and reason, rooted in Scripture and in dialogue with the human sciences, the social teaching of the Church offers reliable guidelines built on reflection and practical wisdom accumulated over centuries. The lives of men and women have offered the world many a practical example of Christian love. Pastors and theologians have given ideas and advice on the nature of Christian fellowship in social life. Over the centuries, the Church has had to address many pressing issues: workers' rights, the evils of totalitarianism, massive disregard for human dignity and rights, the onslaught of the technocratic paradigm, economic and financial crises, destruction of the natural environment, human trafficking and forced migration, and too many others.

The Compendium of the Social Doctrine of the Church covers many such issues, and this makes it a very useful reference for whoever desires to know the Christian social message. However, because of its length and the unavoidable complexity of some passages, it can be daunting for those beginning to learn about the social doctrine of the Church. Besides, since its appearance in 2004, there have been new encyclicals and other documents that deserve a place in any summary of the Church's social teaching. This reflects the fact that new topics and challenges emerge constantly and require an answer rooted in faith.

I am therefore delighted that Prof. Mons. Martin Schlag has edited this *Handbook of Catholic Social Teaching*. It is a *catependium* in the sense that it summarizes the Compendium and preserves its range of contents (*...pendium*), and it adopts the question-and-answer approach of catechisms (*cate...*) that has proven very effective for teaching. This helps the presentation to be amenable and accessible to young people as well as others.

As a consultor to the Pontifical Council for Justice and Peace, Mons. Martin Schlag has witnessed some of the debates in our council and stayed in close contact with us while writing the book. This was especially important for the coverage of the new pontifical documents and new themes which the 2004 Compendium could not have discussed. Discussion of these are highlighted as "special topics."

I hope this *catependium* will be widely read and made available to many people all over the world. Most of all, however, I hope and pray that its contents will move many hearts to respond to the stirrings of the Holy Spirit, and open us to the needs of our brothers and sisters and of the Earth, our common home.

Preface

At the Last Judgment the Lord will ask us what we have done for the poor, the hungry, the sick and the naked, those in prison, and those without a home. What you hold in your hands is not just an academic handbook, but a handbook for your life in the world. Christians throughout the centuries have sought to put into practice Christ's command to love our neighbor, and over time the Church has formulated a social teaching to aid us in this great task. However, this teaching cannot remain theory alone. I challenge you to approach this book like an examination of conscience, meditating on its content and what it means for your life: How can I live out Christ's message of active charity? What do His words mean for me here and now? What would Jesus do if He were in my place?

The task of formulating a social teaching for the whole world is anything but easy. The regional differences, and even more so those between continents, are considerable. People in some parts of the world suffer famine and malnutrition, while in others they have every material thing, but still feel unhappy. In some countries, Christians are persecuted and put to death, while in other countries with religious freedom, some Christians fail to exercise their political rights and to actively participate in social life. Needless to say, the list of differences could go on and on. Notwithstanding the recognition of these differences, the Church, over the centuries, through many painful experiences, has elucidated a number of principles that apply to every society: human dignity, the common good, solidarity, and subsidiarity. She then strives to make them as fruitful as possible for the realities of social life, which are studied and described by the social sciences.

In his concluding address during the last session of the Second Vatican Council, Blessed Paul VI characterized the council's spirituality with "the old story of the [good] Samaritan," which had been "the model of the spirituality of the council." In the council, the Church has inclined herself toward humanity and its needs with "boundless sympathy," and "has, so to say, declared herself the servant of humanity," proposing a "new type of humanism" centered on God the Father, Christ, and the Holy Spirit.[1] It is this Christian or integral humanism that the social teaching of the Church sets forth.

The Second Vatican Council's Pastoral Constitution *Gaudium et Spes* is an outstanding embodiment of this new Christian humanism. In it, the Church enters into dialogue with the world. In a dialogue, both parties give and receive. The Church accepts and receives the values, aims, and achievements of human activity in the world. At the same time, the Church offers the world the light of the Word of God, in which the meaning and the sense of all reality become comprehensible. Man without God ultimately becomes inhuman. We cannot build a society worthy of man without God, as the atheist regimes of the twentieth century have painfully proven. That is why the Church cannot ever interrupt or opt out of this dialogue.

The division into general principles and specific concerns underlies the structure of *Gaudium et Spes*, as well as that of the *Compendium of the Social Doctrine of the Church*, which follows *GS* in the topics it addresses in its second part: the family, labor, economic and political life, peace, ecology, etc. We can therefore apply to the *Compendium* (and also its summary in this book) the explanation given by the council of its Pastoral Constitution: the subject matter which is described in the second, specific part is made up of diverse elements. Some elements have a permanent value; others, only a transitory one. Consequently, the constitution must be interpreted according to the general norms of theological interpretation. Interpreters must bear in mind the changeable circumstances which the subject matter, by its very nature, involves.[2]

The *Compendium* was published in 2004 and since then it has been translated into more than thirty languages. It has proved to be a useful pastoral instrument for spreading the Church's social teaching. Pope Francis has repeatedly referred to the *Compendium* as a secure guide, and it has been put onto the resource library of the Vatican's website among the fundamental texts of the Magisterium. In order to make its contents more accessible, we offer here a summary in the form of a catechism. We have also included new documents of the popes' social teaching. The chapters and their content faithfully correspond to those of the *Compendium*. At the same time, we have tried to summarize the text and to reformulate it in order to make it more comprehensible to a wider audience, Christians and non-Christians alike. This in some cases has meant changing the order in which the paragraphs are presented in the *Compendium*. Through our project, we hope to have fulfilled the wish of St. John Paul II, formulated in a document addressing the special needs of America: "it would be very useful to have a compendium or approved synthesis of Catholic social doctrine, including a 'Catechism,' which would show the connection between it and the new evangelization."[3] A grateful remembrance also goes to St. Josemaría, so closely linked to the academic institutions in which we work, who always desired a catechism setting out the social rights and duties of Christians.

As editor I wish to thank the Pontifical Council for Justice and Peace, its President Peter K.A. Cardinal Turkson, Dr. Flaminia Giovanelli, and Fr. Michael Czerny for their unwavering support of this project. I thank The Catholic University of America Press, especially John B. Martino and Gregory Black for their precise work, and I also thank the CCD and USCCB for permission to quote verbatim the *New American Bible* and the English translation of the *Compendium of the Social Doctrine of the Church,* respectively. (It should be noted that, when the Bible is quoted within the Compendium or another Church document, we use the translation found in the document, not the NAB). Throughout our text, the original italics found in the *Compendium* have been removed, and capitalization for the first word of a sentence has been altered without note. Spelling has also been adjusted to Standard American English.

I extend my gratitude to my colleagues Arturo Bellocq, Gregorio Guitián, and Jennifer E. Miller for writing chapters, and also Pau Agulles, Antonio Malo, Norberto González, and Tebaldo Vinciguerra for their contributions. A very special acknowledgment goes to Elizabeth Reichert: not only has she contributed by writing several sections, but without her patient and diligent work of editing this book would never have been accomplished.

Martin Schlag
Rome, May 1st, 2016, Feast Day of St. Joseph the Worker

Abbreviations

LG   Vatican Council II, Dogmatic Constitution *Lumen
       Gentium*, 1964
LS   Francis, Encyclical Letter *Laudato Si'*, 2015
LW   John Paul II, *Letter to Women*, 1995
MM   John XXIII, Encyclical Letter *Mater et Magistra*, 1961
MV   Francis, Bull *Misericordiae Vultus*, 2015
MW   CDF, *Letter to the Bishops of the Catholic Church on the
       Collaboration of Men and Women in the Church and in
       the World*, 2004
PCJP   Pontifical Council for Justice and Peace
PP   Paul VI, Encyclical Letter *Populorum Progressio*, 1967
PT   John XXIII, Encyclical Letter *Pacem in Terris*, 1963
QA   Pius XI, Encyclical Letter *Quadragesimo Anno*, 1931
SRS   John Paul II, Encyclical Letter *Sollicitudo Rei Socialis*, 1987
STh   Saint Thomas Aquinas, *Summa Theologiae*
USCCB   United States Conference of Catholic Bishops
VBL   PCJP, *Vocation of the Business Leader*, 2012
YC   *Youcat*, 2011

Introduction: *Toward a Christian Humanism*

MARTIN SCHLAG

1. What is the social teaching of the Church?

The social teaching of the Church applies the gospel to our life in society. As human beings and as Christians we are responsible for the world we live in, for the well-being of the people with whom we share this planet, and for the way we organize society. The Christian faith has a social dimension. Speaking of the final judgment, Jesus says that we will be judged by our social works (cf. Mt 25:31–46). This has moved Christians to reflect on their social responsibility. Motivated by this task, the pastors of the Church have developed guiding principles for the Church's social teaching.

The teaching consists of documents published primarily by the popes, but also by episcopal conferences on the consequences of the faith for our life in society. The social teaching of the Church is part of the official teaching of the Catholic Church.

There is also "Catholic social thought," which is a broader concept, and includes the reflections of theologians, other lay people, and workers in the social field.

(CSDC 7–10)

2. What is the *Compendium of the Social Doctrine of the Church?*

As the title indicates, the *Compendium* offers a complete overview or framework of the body of Catholic social teaching. The document is meant to be used for formation, moral discernment, and inspiration and guidance for social action. In short, it summarizes and explains the Church's social teaching, making it accessible to all.

(CSDC 8–10)

3.   Does everything in the *Compendium* (and therefore also in this book) have the same weight or importance?

No. The *Compendium* references magisterial texts of varying levels of authority. There are conciliar documents and encyclicals, but also papal addresses and documents from the offices of the Holy See. "In the social doctrine of the Church can be found the principles for reflection, the criteria for judgment and the directives for action which are the starting point for the promotion of an integral and solidary humanism" (CSDC 7). It is the duty of every Christian to apply these principles and criteria to the concrete circumstances of their lives in order to approach them with the gospel spirit. In this process it is important to take into account that the passage of time and the changing of social circumstances will require renewed reflection on the various issues in order to read and respond to the new signs of the times while remaining faithful to the perennial principles of the faith.

(CSDC 7–9)

4.   What is Christian humanism?

Christian humanism is the contribution of the Christian faith to happiness on earth, not only in heaven, and to the development of every man and woman, their communities, and the society in general. The Church proposes a "humanism that is up to the standards of God's plan of love in history, an integral and solidary humanism capable of creating a new social, economic and political order, founded on the dignity and freedom of every human person, to be brought about in peace, justice and solidarity" (CSDC 19).

(CSDC 18–19)

5.   What does Christian humanism have to do with the Church's social teaching?

Christian humanism is the very aim of the Church's social teaching: the transmission of this solidary and integral humanism, which is fully realized in the light of Jesus Christ, God-made-man. The Church responds to the deepest questions of human existence, of man's place in nature, society, and history. "The direction that human existence, society and history will take depends largely on the answers given to the questions of man's place in nature and society; the purpose of the present document is to make a contribution to these answers" (CSDC 15).

(CSDC 14–15)

1 Charity: *The Heart of Catholic Social Teaching*

ELIZABETH REICHERT

Charity is at the heart of the Church's social doctrine. Every responsibility and every commitment spelt out by that doctrine is derived from charity.

BENEDICT XVI, CARITAS IN VERITATE, 2

We begin with love because it is love, more than justice, that is capable of transforming the relationships among human beings. And it is love that moves a person to work for peace and justice. Love means desiring the good for another and working to bring about that good, which also includes the common good: "The more we strive to secure a common good corresponding to the real needs of our neighbors, the more effectively we love them" (CV 7).

6.   Does love, or more specifically charity, work against achieving justice? Doesn't charity serve to maintain the status quo?

Some argue that charity actually works against justice; it soothes the consciences of the rich by offering temporary solutions to the poor without seeking to remove the underlying causes, thus continuing the cycle of injustice. While there is some truth to this argument, there are also grave errors. One cannot ignore the present, immediate needs of the impoverished in the hope of building a just society. "One does not make the world more human by refusing to act humanely here and now" (DCE 31).

Furthermore, there will never be such a just ordering of society that love somehow becomes superfluous, because love offers more than just material help. "Love—*caritas*—will always prove necessary, even in the most just society.... Whoever wants to eliminate love is preparing to eliminate man as such. There will always be suffering which cries out for consolation and help. There will always be lone-liness…. There will never be a situation where the charity of each individual Christian is unnecessary, because in addition to justice man needs, and will always need, love" (DCE 28–29).

(DCE 26–30; CV 6)

7.   What, then, is the relationship between charity and justice?

"Not only is justice not extraneous to charity, not only is it not an alternative or parallel path to charity: justice is inseparable from charity, and intrinsic to it. Justice is the primary way of charity or, in Paul VI's words, 'the minimum measure' of it"[1] (CV 6).

Justice means giving another his or her due. Charity means offer-ing what is "mine" to the other. Thus, charity goes beyond justice, but it never lacks justice. If I love others, I must first be just towards them; I must first give them what is theirs according to justice.

(CV 6)

8.   What is the relationship between charity and truth?

St. Paul preaches the necessity of *veritas in caritate*, truth in love (cf. Eph 4:15). Without charity, the preaching of the truth becomes overly harsh and cold. However, the inverse is equally important—*caritas in veritate*, love in truth. "Without truth, charity degener-ates into sentimentality. Love becomes an empty shell, to be filled in an arbitrary way" (CV 3). As noted above, charity is at the heart of the social doctrine of the Church, but this charity must always be enlightened by truth. "'*Caritas in veritate*' is the principle around which the Church's social doctrine turns" (CV 6).

(CV 1–6)

9.   Looking at the Old Testament, what was different about God's revelation to the people of Israel?

In God's progressive self-revelation to humanity, His revelation to Israel stands out because He reveals Himself as a personal God with a personal love for His people. He hears and responds to the cries of His people. "I have witnessed the affliction of my people in Egypt and have heard their cry against their taskmasters, so I know well what they are suffering. Therefore I have come down to rescue them from the power of the Egyptians" (Ex 3:7-8).

(CSDC 21; DCE 9)

10. What does the Old Testament teach about social relationships?

The Torah teaches not only fidelity to God, but also addresses the social relations among the people of Israel. The Ten Commandments in particular illuminate man's essential duties, and thus indirectly, his fundamental rights. The prophets call for an internalization of the teachings of the Law, making possible a progressive universalization of these attitudes of justice and solidarity so that they extend to all people.

(CSDC 22-25; DCE 9)

11. What is the novelty of the New Testament in God's revelation of love for humanity?

Jesus "proclaims: 'He who has seen me has seen the Father' (Jn 14:9). Jesus, in other words, is the tangible and definitive manifestation of how God acts towards men and women" (CSDC 28). The novelty of the New Testament is not so much in an idea, but in the person of Christ, who reveals the love of the Father, and reveals that we are all called to be children in the Spirit, and therefore brothers and sisters.

(CSDC 28-31, 33-37; DCE 12)

12. At the center of Jesus's teaching is the twofold commandment of love of God and neighbor; but can love be "commanded"?

Sentiments come and go, but the revelation of God's love in Christ makes it clear that love is not merely a sentiment. Jesus is not demanding of us a feeling, and He does not impose upon us an external, arbitrary commandment. "Since God has first loved us (cf. 1 Jn 4:10), love is now no longer a mere 'command'; it is the response to the gift of love with which God draws near to us" (DCE 1).

(CSDC 32; DCE 1, 17-18)

13. To whom exactly does the "love of neighbor" extend?

The parable of the Good Samaritan universalizes the love of neighbor, thereby abolishing any national or geographical limits. Jesus teaches that every human being must be treated as another self, even if he or she is an enemy (cf. Mt 5:43-44). The love of neighbor extends to every human being and to all social levels; it "must inspire, purify and elevate all human relationships in society and in politics" (CSDC 33).

(CSDC 33, 40; DCE 14-15)

14. But, practically speaking, among the billions of people on the planet, how do I identify "my neighbor"?

Because of the phenomenon of globalization, we are able to know almost instantly of the needs of others even in the most remote regions. This calls for a new readiness to help, now that our charitable activity can and should extend to our brothers and sisters all over the world. At the same time, we cannot allow this awareness of the problems throughout the world to lead to a sort of paralysis in which, overwhelmed by vast suffering, we resign ourselves to doing nothing.

"Anyone who needs me, and whom I can help, is my neighbor. The concept of 'neighbor' is now universalized, yet it remains concrete. Despite being extended to all mankind, it is not reduced to a generic, abstract and undemanding expression of love, but calls for my own practical commitment here and now" (DCE 15).

(CSDC 33, 40; DCE 15, 30-31)

15. We are called to love our neighbor, but what about ourselves?

"You shall love your neighbor *as yourself*" (Mk 12:31, italics added). Love of God and neighbor, then, is not a depreciation of one's self. Persons who themselves are transformed by love are able to transform society. One must attend to his or her own needs—material, social, and especially spiritual. There is a "priority of the conversion of heart" (CSDC 42, quoting CCC 1888) in the path to bringing about social change, a path that requires grace. "The inner transformation of the human person, in his being progressively conformed to Christ, is the necessary prerequisite for a real transformation of his relationships with others" (CSDC 42).

(CSDC 41–44)

16. What effect does the Christian understanding of salvation have on our approach to social action?

Christians believe in a new and eternal dwelling place that is prepared for every human person—a new earth where justice abides. "This hope, rather than weaken, must instead strengthen concern for the work that is needed in the present reality" (CSDC 56). Far from leading to passivity, this truth instills in Christians a longing for a foretaste in this world of what will be fully realized in the world to come. Furthermore, we believe that the salvation of Jesus Christ is offered to all people and to the whole person, in all of his or her dimensions. Christ redeems not only the individual person but also the social relations existing between men and women. Christ not only gave us an example to follow, but He has also transformed each of us into a new creation, and as a new creation, we are then enabled by grace to "live in newness of life" (Rom 6:4).

(CSDC 38–41, 52–58)

17. Does this mean that we are to expect to achieve the fullness of this salvation, the redemption of social relations, in the present age?

This salvation begins to be made a reality already in history; however, we recognize that its completion is in the future. It is characterized by an "eschatological relativity," a sort of "already, but not yet." This means that all cultural, social, economic, and political accomplishments must be understood as relative and provisional realities. "Any totalitarian vision of society and the State, and any purely intra-worldly ideology of progress are contrary to the integral truth of the human person and to God's plan in history" (CSDC 48).

(CSDC 38–39, 48)

2 What is Catholic Social Teaching in the Mission of the Church?

ARTURO BELLOCQ

For I was hungry and you gave me food, I was thirsty and you gave me drink, a stranger and you welcomed me, naked and you clothed me, ill and you cared for me, in prison and you visited me.... Amen, I say to you, whatever you did for one of these least brothers of mine, you did for me.

MT 25:35–40

Throughout the ages, these words have echoed in the consciences of Christians, moving them to open their hearts and reach out their hands to the needs of others. Concern for mankind has led the Church over time to develop a social teaching, which has its own sources, aims, and particular nature.

18. Does the Church have an interest in the concrete history of mankind?

The Church wants the salvation of God to reach each individual, wherever he or she may be; thus she shares in mankind's joys and hopes, anxieties and sadness, and stands in solidarity with every man and woman of every place and time, and brings them the good news of the Kingdom of God.

(CSDC 60; GS 1)

19. Why does the Church have an interest in social relations?

Because social life (and with it politics, the economy, work, law, and culture) often determines the quality of life, and thus the conditions in which every man and woman understands him or herself and makes decisions about his or her vocation, the Church cannot be indifferent to what is decided, brought about or experienced in society; she is attentive to the moral quality—that is, the authentically human and humanizing aspects—of social life.

(CSDC 62)

20. Does the Church have its own message about social relations?

Yes. With the light of faith, the Church has an in-depth knowledge of what it means to be human, our origin and our end, our true happiness, and our weaknesses. This "global perspective on man and human realities" (PP 13) that the Church offers *as her distinctive contribution* sheds light on the complex web of social relations. "She teaches him the demands of justice and peace in conformity with divine wisdom" (CSDC 3, quoting CCC 2419).

(CSDC 3, 63; CCC 2419; PP 13)

21. So, the Church's teaching about social relations forms part of her supernatural mission?

"Christ, to be sure, gave His Church no proper mission in the political, economic or social order. The purpose which He set before her is a religious one" (GS 42). But out of this religious mission a light and an energy emerge which can serve to structure the human community according to the divine law. The supernatural and the natural are not two exclusively separate entities. "The supernatural is not to be understood as an entity or a place that begins where the natural ends, but as the raising of the natural to a higher plane. In this way nothing of the created or the human order is foreign to or excluded from the supernatural or theological order of faith and grace, rather it is found within it, taken on and elevated by it" (CSDC 64).

(CSDC 64; GS 42)

22. Is the social teaching of the Church concerned with all aspects of social life?

No. The social teaching has its *own competency, which is that of proclaiming Christ the Redeemer.* This means that the Church's social teaching does not intervene in technical questions—which correspond to the human sciences—nor does she propose or establish concrete systems or models of social organization. Still less does the Church take on the political task of bringing about the most just society possible. Building a just society—in all its technical complexity—is the mission of politics, not the Church. However, the vision of man and his true good in Christ that the Church possesses through the faith is an important contribution to a "purification of reason," (DCE 28) enabling the demands of justice to be recognized and put into practice.

(CSDC 68; DCE 28)

23. What right does the Church have to announce a social teaching?

The Church has not only the right but also the duty to proclaim her social teaching. It is an integral part of the mission that Christ entrusted to her—to be *teacher of the truth of faith*. This truth that the Church announces not only includes dogma, but also moral truth—including those truths about just social order—that proceed from the gospel and from human nature itself. These truths are necessary for the salvation of man and his happiness on earth.

(CSDC 69–70; DH 14; CIC 747, §2)

24. Is the social teaching of the Church a simple or complex body of teachings?

The social teaching of the Church was not initially considered to be an organic, systematic set of teachings. It has been formed over time through numerous interventions by the Magisterium on social issues. For this reason, it constitutes a *"rich and complex"* body of doctrine (John Paul II, *Address in Puebla, Mexico* 1979, III.7), in which principles of permanent value are mixed with teachings of a more transitory nature that responded to urgent needs at a particular moment. This fact requires an attentive discernment when determining to what degree a teaching forms part of the social doctrine of the Church.

(CSDC 72)

25. Is Catholic social teaching an ideology?

Because of the particular circumstances of its formation—many times characterized by confrontation with opposing conceptions of man and his social life—some confuse Catholic social teaching with an ideology, in the sense of a concrete proposal like other social projects. The Magisterium has made clear that the Church's social teaching does not belong to the category of ideology, nor is it a "third way" between capitalism and socialism, but it is rather *theology*. It is the proclamation of the truth of faith illuminating the ultimate meaning of social realities, and reveals the demands made by the respect due to the human person.

(CSDC 72; SRS 41)

26. So what exactly is the social teaching of the Church?

The social teaching of the Church is "the *accurate formulation* of the results of a careful reflection on the complex realities of human existence, in society and in the international order, in the light of faith and of the Church's tradition. Its main aim is to *interpret* these realities, determining their conformity with or divergence from the lines of the gospel teaching on man and his vocation, a vocation which is at once earthly and transcendent; its aim is thus to *guide* Christian behavior" (CSDC 72, quoting SRS 41).

(CSDC 72; SRS 41)

27. What are the sources of Catholic social teaching?

As in other areas of theology, the sources of Catholic social teaching are Revelation and human nature, especially in its social dimension. Faith *guides* reason in its search for a way to organize a society worthy of man; but faith *does not substitute for reason* in reason's task of understanding the basic concepts and specific dynamics of the distinct areas of social life, which fall under the disciplines of philosophy and the various social sciences.

(CSDC 74–75)

28. So the Church's social teaching enters into dialogue with the social sciences?

Yes. The social teaching needs the social sciences in order to have a proper understanding of its object—the various social realities. The Church's social teaching respects the legitimate autonomy of earthly realities and the various human sciences that study them. However, it invites them to open themselves to a fuller truth, known by faith, so that they can find their ultimate meaning and contribute to the authentic development of man.

(CSDC 76; GS 36)

29. What do we mean by "legitimate autonomy of earthly realities"?

We mean that created things and earthly affairs have their own laws and values which must be respected. This does not mean that they are independent of God and the gospel message. There are moral limits, which are always binding. "For without the Creator the creature would disappear" (GS 36). For instance, markets have their own laws, for example the law of supply and demand; they are, however, subject to God's moral law.

(CSDC 45; GS 36)

30. Does Catholic social teaching propose its own social, political, or economic doctrine?

No. Revelation does not propose any sort of political, economic, or social system at the level of the social sciences that the Church should teach or promote. In these fields, faith invites reason to honestly and diligently investigate the causes of and best solutions for problems. Faith guides reason with its fundamental principles concerning man and his social dimension. These principles serve as a guide, without proposing concrete answers that, in many cases, are contingent from the point of view of the human sciences.

(CSDC 72)

31. Who formulates the Church's social doctrine?

As with other areas of Christian teaching, the Church herself, as the custodian of Revelation, formulates and teaches the social doctrine. Each member of the ecclesial community—priests, religious, lay people, theologians, scientists, and pastors—contributes according to his or her own charism and ministry. However, only the Magisterium is competent to teach the social doctrine with authority. In this case, the doctrinal weight of the various teachings depends on the nature of the teachings, their contingent and variable elements, and the frequency with which they have been invoked.

(CSDC 79–80)

32. Are there both perennial and contingent elements in the Church's social teaching?

Perhaps more than in any other area of theology, the Church's social teaching intertwines various perennial or lasting principles— pertaining to Revelation and to man's immutable nature—with contingent applications. This is because the cultural, political, and economic circumstances in which the Church announces her message are constantly changing. Furthermore, the Church—along with humanity—continues to grow in her understanding of complex social realities and of the specific contribution offered by the gospel (cf. Benedict XVI, *Christmas Address to the Roman Curia* 2005). This characteristic specific to social teaching requires careful discernment on the part of those who receive it; but, far from being a disadvantage, it is a sign of the teaching's capacity for renewal while maintaining its fundamental principles.

(CSDC 80, 85–86; SRS 3; DonVer 24)

33. What are the tasks of proclamation and denunciation in Catholic social teaching?

Because of her profound knowledge of man, the Church has a special sensibility for recognizing violations of the dignity of the person and social groups, and must make her voice heard in defense of the most vulnerable. But prior to this task of *denunciation*, the

Church must *proclaim* the truth of man and society that she possesses as her own, and then must proclaim the norms and directives of action that derive from them. With this teaching, the Church does not attempt to structure or organize society, but to appeal to, guide, and form consciences.

(CSDC 81)

34. Who receives Catholic social teaching?

All members of the Church receive her social teaching. Each of the faithful, according to his or her vocation, must contribute to the building of a more just society. In a special way, this teaching is directed to lay people because it involves responsibilities related to the building, organizing, and functioning of society: political, economic, and administrative obligations that pertain to lay people in virtue of the secular nature of their vocation, and not to priests or religious. The light of faith does not undermine the rational power of the Church's social teaching, and it is therefore also directed toward all men and women of good will who are outside the Church.

(CSDC 83)

35. When lay people work to permeate social realities with a Christian spirit, do they act in the name of the Church?

No, when lay people order earthly realities according to the spirit of the gospel, they do not do so in name of the Church, but as citizens of the State, according to their own responsibilities. The Church, because of her religious mission, is not tied to any political or economic system. Sometimes "the Christian view of things will itself suggest some specific solution in certain circumstances. Yet it happens rather frequently, and legitimately so, that with equal sincerity some of the faithful will disagree with others on a given matter" (GS 43). Given the contingency of social matters, there will always be a legitimate plurality of temporal options for lay people, that is, always within the limits of Christian morality.

(DCE 29; GS 43, 76)

36. When was Catholic social teaching born?

The Church has always demonstrated her concern for social matters and offered guidance concerning ever-changing historical realities. Drawing from Revelation, and owing to the teachings of the Fathers and the Doctors of the Church, a rich heritage of Christian social morality has been formed over time. The economic and political events of the nineteenth century, however, transformed society in such a way that a new effort of discernment of the fundamental principles of the social order was necessary. Leo XIII's emblematic encyclical *Rerum Novarum* is considered the beginning of this new organic and synthetic way of confronting social problems.

(CSDC 87–88; John Paul II, *General Audience* May 13, 1981)

37. What are the central points of the social magisterium of Leo XIII?

In his numerous social and political encyclicals, Leo XIII explained the Christian teaching on temporal power and its relationship to religious power, stated his judgment on the new forms of government and social organization, and offered criteria for the participation of Christians in public life. Many of these teachings contain contingent elements specific to the circumstances and mentality of the time, but as a whole, these documents express the fundamental principles of the faith in social matters. The encyclical *Rerum Novarum* is especially important. It studies in depth the *labor question*, brought to the fore by the economic and political revolutions of the nineteenth century. The document outlines the errors of this period that resulted in certain social ills. It rules out socialism as a remedy and sets forth a number of teachings regarding work, law, and property: the principle of collaboration instead of class struggle as the means to social change; the rights of the weak; the dignity of the poor and the obligations of the rich; the perfection of justice in charity; and the right to form professional associations.

(CSDC 89)

38. What did the teachings of Pius XI contribute to Catholic social teaching?

Pius XI was forced to confront grave political and economic crises during his pontificate, and he responded with several important documents. Shortly after the serious economic crisis of 1929, he published the encyclical *Quadragesimo Anno* (1931) to commemorate the fortieth anniversary of *Rerum Novarum*. In this encyclical, he developed Christian social principles at a time when industrialization coincided with the expansion of the national and international power of financial entities. The encyclical rejects both materialistic socialism and the liberal ideology of the times and re-affirms the value of private property, insisting on its social value. The encyclical's teachings on the *principle of subsidiarity* and the notion of a just wage are of particular importance. Furthermore, Pius XI never ceased speaking out against the totalitarian regimes that took hold in Europe during his pontificate. In 1931 he protested against the atrocities of the fascist regime in Italy with publication of the encyclical *Non Abbiamo Bisogno* ("We Do Not Need"). In 1937, in the encyclical *Mit Brennender Sorge* ("With Burning Anxiety"), he rejected the Nazi ideology and the Nazi regime's repressive measures. In the same year he also promulgated the encyclical *Divini Redemptoris* on atheistic communism.

(CSDC 91–92)

39. What characterizes the social magisterium of Pius XII?

Pius XII was responsible for guiding the Church during the Second World War and afterward during reconstruction of the social order. While he did not write any social encyclicals, he consistently demonstrated his concern over upheavals in the international order. In his many speeches and radio messages on social issues, he emphasized the need for a harmonious relationship between law and morality so that a just social order can be constructed at national and international levels. Additionally, in his many encounters with people across various social classes and professional societies, he provided concrete guidance on ways of contributing to the common good.

(CSDC 93)

40.   What were the central characteristics of John XXIII's pontificate in the area of social teaching?

With his personality and his teaching, John XXIII promoted the universal dissemination of Catholic social teaching, in dialogue with all men and women of good will. In years marked by recovery after the war, the beginning of decolonization, and the first signs of dialogue between the American and Soviet blocs, John XXIII showed himself capable of reading "the *signs of the times* and of interpreting them in the light of the Gospel" (GS 4, italics added). He wrote two social encyclicals. The first, *Mater et Magistra* (1961), updates the social teaching of *Rerum Novarum* for a context in which social problems had become universalized, and speaks to certain concrete problems including agriculture, relations between poor and rich countries, and the demographic problem. The second, *Pacem in Terris* (1963), addresses the conditions for promoting national and international peace, and the need to respect human rights.

(CSDC 94–95)

41.   What was the importance of the Second Vatican Council for Catholic social teaching?

The council was a moment of great importance for Catholic social teaching; it brought about a profound reflection on the mission of the Church in the world, and therefore also on her contribution to the solution of social problems. The pastoral constitution *Gaudium et Spes* outlines the face of a Church that is "truly linked with mankind and its history" (GS 1). The Church walks with humanity and together they are subject to the same earthly circumstances; but at the same time the Church serves "as a leaven and as a kind of soul for human society as it is to be renewed in Christ and transformed into God's family" (GS 40). *Gaudium et Spes* offers a systematic presentation on culture, economic and social life, marriage and family, the political community, and peace and the community of nations—all in the light of Christian anthropology and the Church's mission. Another important council document in the body of Catholic social teaching is the declaration *Dignitatis Humanae*, in which the right to religious freedom is clearly proclaimed, accompanied by important clarifications on the relationship between religion and political power.

(CSDC 96–97)

42. What were Paul VI's contributions to Catholic social teaching?

Paul VI wrote two important social documents. In the encyclical *Populorum Progressio* (1967), he explained the Christian teaching on authentic social development—which must be comprehensive, fostering "the development of each man and of the whole man" (PP 14)—and urged those in power to act in solidarity with the most vulnerable. In the same year, the Pope established the Pontifical Council of Justice and Peace "to stimulate the Catholic community to promote progress in needy regions and international social justice" (CSDC 99, quoting GS 90). Later, in the apostolic letter *Octogesima Adveniens* (1971), in the midst of strong ideological controversies inside and outside the Church, he reflected on post-industrial society with its many complex problems, underlining the inadequacy of current ideologies in responding to the challenges of the day: urbanization, the condition of young people, the status of women, unemployment, discrimination, emigration, population growth, the influence of the media, and the ecological problem.

(CSDC 98–100)

43. What were John Paul II's most important social documents?

John Paul II's long and fruitful pontificate was rich in contributions to social questions, including three social encyclicals. *Laborem Exercens* (1981) focuses on human work as being key to the entire social question. Human work cannot be reduced to its objective and material aspects, but should be considered as the place where one's personal, natural, and supernatural vocation is realized. *Sollicitudo Rei Socialis* (1987) returns to the topic of development in order to set out its moral implications and the moral obligations it imposes on people in the contemporary world; it outlines the Christian and human meaning of solidarity among various countries and social groups, and also explains in detail the nature of Catholic social teaching as a theological discipline. Lastly, *Centesimus Annus* (1991), written to commemorate the 100-year anniversary of *Rerum Novarum*, offers an analysis of the fall of communism and an in-depth explanation of the advantages of democracy and the free economy while highlighting the risks that these present when they are not based on an adequate anthropology.

(CSDC 101–103)

44. **What are the most relevant teachings that Benedict XVI has left us in social matters?**

Benedict XVI wrote a social encyclical, *Caritas in Veritate* (2009), in which he analyzed the causes of society's profound cultural crisis and proposed a new *Christian humanism*, centered on charity as the fundamental criterion of all social relations. On numerous occasions he reflected on the Church's mission in society and the contribution that faith offers to social problems, particularly by assisting reason, often threatened by relativism, in perceiving ethical obligations.

45. **What are the main features of Pope Francis's teaching on social issues?**

In word and in deed, Pope Francis has worked to promote, both inside and outside the Church, a greater awareness of the grave social and cultural problems of our time, calling all people of good will to their personal and societal responsibilities. Evangelical poverty, characterized by a detachment from material goods, and attention to the most needy, are two criteria that must always be present in a society aspiring to be worthy of man. In his social encyclical *Laudato Si'*, the Pope addresses many contemporary issues with the idea of an "integral ecology" which respects all human and social dimensions. Against the current individualistic cultures, this ecology recognizes that everything is connected, and therefore our decisions must be based on ecological, social, and economic concerns together with an awareness of our common origin, our mutual belonging, and our responsibility toward future generations.

3 The Dignity of the Human Person as the Core and Foundation of Catholic Social Teaching

MARTIN SCHLAG

> God created mankind in his image;
>   in the image of God he created them;
>   male and female he created them.
> God blessed them and God said to them: Be fertile and multiply; fill
> the earth and subdue it. Have dominion over the fish of the sea, the
> birds of the air, and all the living things that crawl on the earth.
>
> GEN 1:27–28

Every human person is created in God's image, endowed with
dignity and inalienable rights and also duties. The human person
is both the foundation and goal of society, and thus it is the principal
task of every society to defend and foster human dignity in its laws
and institutions.

46. What is human dignity?

Human dignity is the first and most important of all social principles. This quality that is inherent in every human being can also be
expressed in the idea that each human person possesses certain
inalienable rights from the moment of conception. In practice, dignity means that no human being is to be degraded and reduced to
a mere means or a tool for ends that are foreign to his or her own
personal development. In particular, the human person's life and
dignity must not be sacrificed for the sake of scientific research, or
economic, military, social, or political goals.

(CSDC 133)

47. Does human dignity only forbid degrading others?

No. This is only the core or minimum expression of human dignity. This core entails the protection of every person against degrading treatment by other individuals or by society as a whole. Human dignity in this sense cannot be lost, not even by the worst criminal. This is because human dignity is not earned or granted by others but is simply possessed. Beyond this, human dignity also has a positive dimension, which is its maximum or moral expression: every human being has a calling to moral excellence and should strive to flourish by expressing his or her dignity through a virtuous life. This means, in turn, that we can act beneath our dignity, thus disfiguring it. In this sense, human dignity is more about living virtuously than possessing rights.

(CSDC 133–134)

48. Before we can think about the consequences of human dignity for social ethics, we must understand the definition of a "society." What is a society?

"A *society* is a group of persons bound together organically by a principle of unity that goes beyond each one of them. As an assembly that is at once visible and spiritual, a society endures through time: it gathers up the past and prepares for the future" (CCC 1880). Put simply, a society is a group of people who are united by a common good.

(CCC 1880)

49. Why do societies come into existence?

People join together in a society out of common utility and friendship. "It is out of love for one's own good and for that of others that people come together in stable groups with the purpose of attaining a common good" (CSDC 150). Some "societies, such as the family and the state, correspond more directly to the nature of man; they are necessary to him" (CCC 1882). However, society can also become oppressive or even totalitarian. That is why the Church teaches that public laws must be in accordance with God's will, the only true source of our freedom. The Church also underscores the principle of subsidiarity in order to avoid oppression. Human beings are not uniform; each one of us pursues happiness in many different ways. This social pluralism is healthy as long as it remains within the limits of God's moral law, which shows us the path to happiness.

(CSDC 150–151)

50. Where does human dignity come from?

Human dignity comes from the fact that every man and woman is the living image of God Himself and called to eternal life. Even though we have disfigured God's image in us through sin, it is not completely destroyed; Christ, the perfect Image of God, has recreated human nature and united it to God in the Holy Spirit.

(CSDC 105)

51. What does it mean to be made in the image of God?

It means that every human being, as frail and unimportant as he or she may appear to human eyes, represents God on earth: "Amen, I say to you, whatever you did for one of these least brothers of mine, you did for me" (Mt 25:40). Each person is a unique and individual being. With every child that is conceived something awesome and wonderful comes into this world; simply by the fact of being, every person has the right to exist.

(CSDC 131)

52. What else can we learn from the Bible about human dignity?

We learn that God created man and woman as individual selves with freedom and responsibility, and at the same time as persons in relationships.

(CSDC 108)

53. What does it mean to be an "individual self"?

Being an individual self means that a human being exists as an "I," capable of self-understanding, self-possession, and self-determination.

The human person is a subjective entity, a bearer of consciousness and freedom, whose unique life experiences are identical to those of no one else. The person, including his or her body, is completely entrusted to him or herself, who is therefore morally responsible for his or her own actions.

(CSDC 127, 131)

54. **Why is relationship so important for us if we are already an individual self?**

Human dignity cannot be explained apart from our relationship to God, other human persons, and creation. Neither our intelligence nor our autonomy, neither our individual selfness nor our personality or personal qualities can sufficiently establish our dignity. The Bible teaches us that the human person was created in relationship with God: we have dignity because we can relate to God as His beloved children. No other creature (except the angels) can do this. The whole of our life and our dignity is essentially and constitutively an answer to God's love. "The human being is a personal being created by God to be in relationship with him; man finds life and self-expression only in relationship, and tends naturally to God"[1] (CSDC 109).

(CSDC 109)

55. **If we are made in the image of God, are we therefore also made in the image of the Holy Trinity?**

Yes. This is expressed by the Bible in that God originally created the human person in the relationship of man and woman: God created the human being as a couple, as a "we" that is called to mutual communion. This "we" is an image of the triune God. In the Holy Trinity each Divine Person gives Himself completely to the other two. In an analogous way, as human beings we discover ourselves as persons with dignity only through the sincere gift of ourselves.

(CSDC 111; CV 53–55)

56. **What about people who are not married? Are they able to live out this calling to relationship?**

Yes. We are relational and social beings by nature. Living in community is a natural characteristic that distinguishes man from other earthly creatures. From the very beginning of his or her existence, the human person is called to life in society. Those who renounce marriage for the Kingdom of God because they have received the calling to celibacy fully realize this call to communion, each according to his or her own vocation, whether as a priest, religious, or layperson.

(CSDC 110, 112–114, 149)

57. The human being is social by nature, but how has sin affected our relationships?

Pride, selfishness, and other sins cause us to close in on ourselves and tempt us to dominate our neighbor. We have all sinned, but we have also all been redeemed by Christ's death and resurrection. Christian realism sees the abysses of sin, but we see them in the light of the hope given by Jesus Christ's act of redemption, in which sin and death are destroyed. This hope is greater than any evil.

(CSDC 120–123, 150)

58. What consequences does sin have for social life?

Sin is a twofold wound affecting man's inmost self and his relationships. At the root of painful personal and social divisions there is always sin. That is why we can speak of sin in its personal and its social dimensions. Every sin is essentially the personal act of an individual; however, a sin is also social when and insofar as it has social consequences. God's healing grace therefore also extends to social life, redeeming human relationships.

(CSDC 116–117)

59. Aren't there also sinful structures or structures of sin that mar human happiness?

Yes. Every sin against the justice we owe others is a social sin. When many repeat these sins, a structure of sin forms and spreads. These structures of sin can become social customs or even laws. The consequences of sin thus perpetuate the structures of sin, which grow stronger and become sources of other sins, conditioning human thought and conduct and opposing it to the will of God and the good of our neighbor. Structures of sin "are rooted in personal sin and, therefore, are always connected to concrete acts of the individuals who commit them, consolidate them and make it difficult to remove them" (CSDC 119).

(CSDC 118–119)

60. How can we overcome structures of sin?

We can overcome structures of sin by courageously opposing and denouncing them, individually and together with others in society. Joint actions are especially necessary to change the culture in which we live and to make an impact on a structural level.

(CSDC 118)

61. What does human dignity mean for social ethics?

Understanding that human dignity is the first and foremost social principle means that we owe each and every human being respect and recognition of his or her personhood. Understanding human dignity also means that such respect and recognition is not a consequence of civil law but is prior to the formation of society. Societies exist in order to protect and to foster human dignity. Every society must accept and defend human dignity through its laws and every other just means available, starting with the protection of innocent life, because dignity is not bestowed on us by any human decision but is a gift of God. The social principle of human dignity also means therefore that the recognition of each and every human being as a person is independent of his or her efforts or merits. Unlike social esteem or prestige, dignity in its core expression is not earned.

(CSDC 153)

62. What does this imply for any society?

A society is just only if and insofar as it is based on respect for the transcendent dignity of the human person. Society is ordered to the human person as its ultimate end.

(CSDC 132)

63. What importance does human dignity have for the social teaching of the Church?

The principle of the inviolable dignity of the human person represents the heart and soul of Catholic social thought. The whole of the Church's social doctrine develops from it, and affirms the centrality of the human person in every sector and expression of society. The human person is its "subject, foundation and goal"[2] (CSDC 106).

(CSDC 106–107)

64. Is the social principle of human dignity universally accepted?

A growing number of constitutions and international agreements proclaim the principle of human dignity. However, it is always endangered by reductionist conceptions of the human person. Some of these are ideological in character or are simply the result of widespread practices. The common denominator of these reductions is that they overemphasize one of the characteristics of man and woman as the image of God at the expense of the other. Thus they either overstress individualism (as in the forms of practical materialism that sacrifice the unborn and the sick to individual desires) or relationality (as in collectivism). The social teaching of the Church maintains the balance between these two characteristics.

(CSDC 124–125)

65. What about the Church's teaching on human dignity—is it not an ideology?

No, the social teaching of the Church is not an ideology because it is based on the truth about man that God has revealed. In the Christian faith God is revealed as the truth (cf. Jn 14:6) that at the same time is love (cf. 1 Jn 4:8). Because truth and love in God are the same, the truth that the Church teaches about man and society must not be imposed by violence. Actually, human dignity as a principle stems more from love than from justice, even though it requires laws to protect it.

(CSDC 126)

66.   What is the Church's task regarding human dignity?

The pastoral task of the Church regarding human dignity is twofold: on the one hand, she proclaims its Christian foundations; on the other, she denounces its violations. Unfortunately, human history is full of the most loathsome and horrible rejections of human dignity. In order to be more effective in her mission, the Church is open "to ecumenical cooperation, to dialogue with other religions, to all appropriate contacts with other organizations, governmental and non-governmental, at the national and international levels. The Church trusts above all in the help of the Lord and his Spirit who, poured forth into human hearts, is the surest guarantee for respecting justice and human rights, and for contributing to peace" (CSDC 159).

(CSDC 159)

67.   What other important social principles form part of the principle of human dignity?

Freedom and equality are part of the social principle of human dignity.

68.   Why is freedom so important in the Christian faith?

Freedom is important in the Christian faith because we can believe in and love God only in freedom. God has given us freedom as one of the highest manifestations of being made in His image.

(CSDC 136)

69.   What is freedom?

We speak of freedom in different ways, and there are actually different types of freedom. On one level, we can speak of being free from physical constraint or from the threat of physical constraint (chains, force, terror, etc.). A second type of freedom is interior and psychological freedom through which we are able to do what we recognize as good without being tied down by disordered passions, addictions, and so on. The highest form of freedom is achieved when the human person realizes his or her calling to self-donation in love. This greatest form of freedom and dignity was realized and revealed by Jesus Christ on the cross.

(CSDC 143; John Paul II, *Angelus Address in Berlin* June 23, 1996)

70. Is there a link between freedom and the moral law?

Yes. Human freedom belongs to us as creatures; it is a freedom that is given as a gift, like a seed that needs to be cultivated. God has given us the moral law as a guideline through which human nature and society flourish. When we presume to be the creators and absolute masters of good and evil, freedom dies, destroying man and society.

(CSDC 138)

71. What does Jesus mean for our freedom?

Jesus truly sets us free. Too often, either intentionally or because of weakness, we commit sins. Human freedom (understood here as self-determination) therefore needs to be liberated. This is done by Christ, who overcame sin and death, calls us to life, and gives us the grace to free ourselves from the disordered love of self.

(CSDC 143)

72. Good actions enhance our freedom. How do we know what is good for the human person and society?

We know what is good and evil because we can recognize the natural moral law through the light of our intellect and, additionally, through God's Revelation. This law is universal because it extends to all people. In its principal precepts, the divine and natural law is presented in the Ten Commandments. It indicates the primary and essential norms regulating moral life in society, and is unchangeable. "Its central focus is the act of aspiring and submitting to God, the source and judge of everything that is good, and also the act of seeing others as equal to oneself. The natural law expresses the dignity of the person and lays the foundations of the person's fundamental duties"[3] (CSDC 140).

(CSDC 140)

73. Aren't there many cultures in the world with different moral
     convictions?

Most cultures adhere to the basic tenets of the natural law; however, not everyone inside or outside those cultures recognizes its
precepts. Therefore God has also revealed it. The natural law, which
is the law of God, cannot be annulled by human sinfulness or by the
majority in a democracy. The natural moral law lays the indispensable moral foundation for any human community and for civil law.
(CSDC 141–142)

74. Why are all human beings equal?

All human beings are equal in the sense that all have the same dignity as creatures made in the image and likeness of God. The fact
that the Son of God took on human nature reinforces this equality
in dignity: "There is neither Jew nor Greek, there is neither slave
nor free person, there is not male and female; for you are all one in
Christ Jesus" (Gal 3:28). The dignity of every person before God is
"the ultimate foundation of the radical equality and brotherhood
among all people, regardless of their race, nation, sex, origin, culture,
or class" (CSDC 144).

(CSDC 144)

75. What does equality mean as a principle for the ordering
     of society?

All people are equal in regard to their dignity and their fundamental
rights but not in regard to their merits, their needs, and their functions. As a social principle and particularly as a legal principle equality does not mean uniformity. In order to be equal and just, laws
must treat different realities according to their differences, and identical realities according to their sameness. A law that treats different
matters in an identical way or identical matters differently is a discriminatory and unjust law. Therefore, equal things must be treated
equally, and different things differently. For example, because of human dignity, every human person's life must be protected. It would

be unjust discrimination to establish differences in this protection because of, for example, a person's age. However, there are some areas where it makes sense to make distinctions regarding such qualities as age. For example, in regard to voting, military service, and other civic duties, distinctions according to age make sense and are not unjust.

76.   But aren't all inequalities unjust?

No. There are many natural inequalities that are not unjust: we are all born with different talents, in different times and places, etc. Additionally, each human person is born into a particular political, economic, and social situation, and therefore inequalities are inevitable to a certain degree. Failure to recognize such inequalities would dampen incentives needed so that certain talents and assets can be employed in the service of the general public. Differing levels of merit and effort expended inevitably produce certain inequalities.

Inequality becomes unjust when it comes about as the result of illegal or immoral practices, unfair methods, favoritism, or cronyism. The job of public authorities and of society at large is to promote conditions of equal opportunity, for example by fostering fair social competition and access to health care and education.

(EG 202)

77.   What about men and women—are they equal?

Yes. Men and women are equal in dignity. At the same time, there exists a certain "difference in equality" between male and female persons. There is something specific and unique to femininity that is different from that which is specific and unique to masculinity. Furthermore, "this difference in equality is enriching and indispensable for the harmony of life in society" (CSDC 146). Ensuring the rightful presence of women in the Church, in the workplace, and in society as a whole is not only a matter of recognizing and promoting their equal dignity, but also of recognizing and promoting that which is specific and unique to them.

(CSDC 146–148)

Special Topic: *Bioethics*

PAU AGULLES

78. Is the protection of life important to human development?

Yes. Life, by its very nature, is the foundation of all other human values, rights, and duties. If life is not respected, if it is violated or its elimination tolerated, then human development becomes impossible. Life is always a good; thus any direct attack against it is always an evil. This is expressed clearly in the commandment: "Thou shall not kill."
(CSDC 155–156; EV 40–41, 52–57)

79. Why is there a duty to preserve human life and health?

This duty follows from the dignity and sanctity of human life and the principle of its inviolability. Health is a good that follows from life and is ordered toward it. Health is ordinarily the necessary condition for our development, including our spiritual development. Caring for one's health and others' is a duty of responsibility toward the lives that have been entrusted to us: our own and those of others. It is a duty toward self, God, and others. However, health care is no longer reasonable when it becomes an end in itself, or leads to worship of the body, or is ordered toward any evil end. The moral responsibility for health and body includes adequate nutrition, clothing, a dignified place to live, hygiene and rest, and proper and proportionate medical care. Public authorities and society in general are also in part responsible for these duties.
(CCC 2288–2289; EV 71)

80. Does it make sense to speak of bioethics as a matter of justice?

Yes. In human relations, the virtue of justice plays a fundamental role. It consists in giving each person and society that which is rightfully theirs. Bioethics deals with a specific type of these relations, that which concerns human life and health. As such, bioethics is not simply a matter of applying a list of norms to specific cases; it is first and foremost a matter of acting justly toward human life.

(EV 13, 57, 66, 101)

81. And abortion, why is it a "social" issue and not just a matter of individual morality?

The impact of legislation and general tolerance of abortion goes beyond each individual case of abortion. Laws and institutions that promote abortion bring with them a diminished respect for life, and therefore for motherhood, and also an attitude of sexual permissiveness. "In this sense abortion goes beyond the responsibility of individuals and beyond the harm done to them, and takes on a distinctly social dimension. It is a most serious wound inflicted on society and its culture" (EV 59). Women often feel pressure to abort from the demands of their careers, from friends, and even from their own families. Promoting social aid for families and mothers in distress is an important measure to counteract these pressures and to contribute to the building of a culture of life.

(EV 26, 59; CV 28; LS 120)

82. What are some of the social and political repercussions of laws like those that permit abortion or euthanasia?

The modern State should have as its primary end the protection of the fundamental good of human life, and thus it has the obligation to guarantee the *absolute* prohibition of its voluntary elimination, even in difficult "borderline" cases. When this good is not respected, as for example in the cases of abortion or euthanasia, the very foundation of the State crumbles, and with it its authority. Moreover, the experience of those countries with a history of legalized abortion and euthanasia provide evidence of what is called the "slippery slope." What begins as an exception in difficult cases has the effect of opening the door to widespread practices, ending in greater abuses against human life.

(EV 72–74; PT 51; CDF, *Declaration on Procured Abortion* 1974, 22)

83.   What does the Church say about suicide?

The Church holds that, like murder, suicide is always morally unacceptable. It is true that there may be certain psychological, cultural, and social conditions that could mitigate or even nullify the person's subjective culpability. However, acknowledgment of this reality should not act as a positive reinforcement of suicide, but rather springs from a deep understanding of the measure of God's love in light of the law, which applies to all sins. Even in the most desperate cases, though, suicide is the destruction of the living image of God. It is the renunciation of love of self and of the duties of justice and of love toward neighbor and society, as well as the denial of God's absolute sovereignty over life and death. This should be distinguished from those cases in which one puts his or her life at risk with the goal of achieving an important or necessary good (e.g., the work of policemen, firemen, and doctors). These cases do not violate the moral law.

(CCC 2281–2283; EV 66; IB I)

84.   Why is the Church opposed to euthanasia?

Euthanasia is a grave violation of God's law because it is the deliberate killing of a human person, whatever the reasons may be or the means that are used to bring it about. Human life and its dignity are intrinsic goods, regardless of the "quality" of life—a sick person has the same dignity as a healthy person. Therefore, its termination is always a moral evil. The legitimate right to self-determination does not extend to life itself but rather to the way one lives that life. Furthermore, as previously noted, the acceptance of euthanasia in select cases is subject to the "slippery slope," leading to abuses and inflicting a grave wound on society, especially on society's attitude toward the sick and dying.

(EV 65; IB)

85.   Does the human embryo deserve the same legal protection as adult humans?

As biology has proven, the human embryo is a complete human being from the moment of conception. Throughout his or her development, all the changes that take place are quantitative (e.g., size, shape, the number of cells, etc.) never qualitative (i.e., a new or different being). From the union of the two gametes, the embryo is a being of the human species that constitutes a new biological being (different from the mother or father, but *like* them), whose growth is continuous and relatively autonomous. It follows that, just as it is illicit to voluntarily eliminate a human life that is already born, it is likewise wrong to eliminate an unborn human life. Constitutions and laws must therefore protect life in the earliest stages of development, especially in the mother's womb, the moment in which human life is most innocent, vulnerable, and dependent.

(EV 58; DonVit I; DP 1–5; CDF, *Declaration on Procured Abortion* 1974, III, V)

86. **What are the main political problems related to abortion?**

The main ethical-political problem posed by the legalization of abortion is that it introduces grave injustice and discrimination. This juridical situation arbitrarily posits that a certain group of human beings (the unborn) be excluded from the group of protected citizens and persons. Society exists to be of service to the human person; thus disregard for the right to life of some human beings is irreconcilably opposed to the possibility of realizing the common good.

(EV 72)

87. **Are there cases in which a Catholic politician can vote in favor of a law that permits abortion?**

If it is not possible to completely repeal an existing law that permits abortion, a politician, clearly and openly stating his or her opposition to abortion, can rightfully support proposals that seek to limit the damage of such a law and reduce its effects on the culture and public morality. In this way, one is not cooperating in the evil of abortion but is making a legitimate attempt to ameliorate the evil aspects of a law (in every way presently possible). The politician must do so in a way that does not cause scandal or confusion.

(EV 73)

88. What is the Church's basic teaching on artificial procreation?

The Church upholds the following fundamental moral principles regarding artificial procreation: (1) first and foremost, any medical intervention must treat the embryo as a person from the moment of conception; (2) human procreation must take place in marriage between one man and one woman, becoming mother and father only through one another, by means of the conjugal act—the loving act that is the only act worthy of bringing a new life into the world; (3) any medical intervention must respect human dignity when it seeks to *assist* the conjugal act to reach its natural end or to enable it to achieve its natural end once it has been normally performed; and (4) the moral gravity of those medical interventions that do not respect these principles is evaluated based on the degree to which they *substitute* for the conjugal act rather than *assisting* it.

(DonVit; DP 12–13)

89. So what kind of reproductive technologies are not in line with Christian morality?

The methods that are not in line with Christian morality include artificial fertilization that takes place outside the body (like IVF and ICSI); artificial heterologous insemination (where the donor is not the spouse); and those homologous methods (where the sperm donor is the spouse) in which the sperm is collected outside the conjugal act.

In addition to the aforementioned moral issues, many of these technologies carry with them further serious problems, including the widespread practice of freezing and storing embryos (cryopreservation), who will either be left to die or used for research; selective reduction of implanted embryos (by means of abortion); eugenic selection; and other attacks against the dignity of the child such as surrogate motherhood, the selling of sperm and eggs, etc.

(DonVit II; DP 14–22)

90. What does the Church say about stem cell research?

Through biotechnology, man exercises his dominion over creation in an excellent way, transforming and ordering his many resources in favor of the dignity and well-being of the human person and the

whole human race. Stem cell research thus deserves respect and encouragement. This new biomedical field has opened the door to
promising results.

Moral issues arise when human life is not respected. This occurs,
in particular, in embryonic stem cell research in which embryos
(usually resulting from methods of artificial reproduction) are
destroyed in order to obtain some of their cells. Use of these cells in
clinical or research settings by third parties involves serious moral
problems because of these parties' cooperation in this evil and participation in "structures of sin."

(DP 31–33; Pontifical Academy for Life, *Declaration on
the Production and the Scientific and Therapeutic Use of Human
Embryonic Stem Cells* 2000)

91. **What does the Church say about medical treatment? Is it
necessary to prolong life at all costs? What about stable
patients that can no longer feed themselves in a natural way?**

Each person has the general moral obligation to care for his or her
own health. The following principles help to clarify the concrete
application of this general principle: (1) no procedure should be
performed in order to directly or intentionally hasten death, meaning that all forms of euthanasia and suicide must be avoided; (2) disproportionate or futile means that cause unnecessary suffering and
offend the person's dignity must be avoided; (3) a patient has a legitimate right to choose whether or not to be subjected to a particular
medical treatment. The refusal of certain treatments does not necessarily equate to euthanasia; rather, it is often an expression of the
acceptance of the human condition when faced with death. Therefore, it is important to distinguish between directly seeking death
and accepting one's naturally approaching death; and (4) a patient
must not refuse or be denied *ordinary and proportionate means* that
are considered "minimal," which are aimed at maintaining life and
providing physical and psychological comfort. The following are
generally considered ordinary and proportionate: nutrition and hydration, respiratory aid, pain relievers, postural changes, and similar
palliative care.

(USCCB, *Q&A Regarding the Holy See's Responses on Nutrition and
Hydration for Patients in a "Vegetative State"* 2007)

92. What are the moral problems posed by organ transplants
    and the sale of organs?

Organ donation is a praiseworthy and generous action that offers
the possibility of health and life to some patients. In order to be
morally licit, it must, however, adhere to the following principles: (1)
any practice that commercializes organs is morally unacceptable; it
uses the body as an object and is a violation of human dignity; (2)
any act of donation requires informed consent; (3) vital organs can
only be extracted *ex cadavere*, that is, from the body of one who is
confirmed dead with moral certitude; and (4) with respect to trans-
plant waiting lists, criteria must be followed that are strictly immu-
nological and clinical and never discriminatory (such as sex, race,
religion, social status, etc.) or utilitarian (such as the ability to work,
the social utility of the patient, etc.).

(EV 86; DP 34–35; John Paul II, *Address to the 18th International
Congress of the Transplantation Society* 2000)

4 The Principles of Catholic Social Teaching

GREGORIO GUITIÁN

> *The Church's social teaching proposes principles for reflection; it provides criteria for judgment; it gives guidelines for action.*
>
> CATECHISM OF THE CATHOLIC CHURCH, 2423

As the Christian community grew and as the social circumstances changed, Christians were called to live up to the challenge of bearing social and political responsibility in society. Their Christian vocation called them to seek guidance in the Bible and in the living Tradition of the Church. There they discovered the principles and values that govern Christian life in society. However, they also understood that in addition to Revelation, reason was necessary in order to apply these principles well. Thus they also developed criteria of practical wisdom and guidelines for action.

93. What are the permanent or fundamental principles of Catholic social teaching?

The fundamental or permanent principles of Catholic social teaching are the principle of the *dignity of the human person,* which is the foundation of all other principles of Catholic social teaching, the principle of the *common good,* the principle of *subsidiarity,* and the principle of *solidarity.*

(CSDC 160)

94. What are the characteristics of these principles?

The fundamental principles of Catholic social teaching have four characteristics: (1) they have a *permanent value* although social circumstances change; (2) they refer to the "ultimate and organizational foundations of life in society" (CSDC 163), making these principles *the basis for the entire social teaching* because they refer to the social reality as a whole: politics, economics, law, relations among various communities, and international relations; (3) the principles form a *unity* that does not allow for one to be understood apart from the others—among the principles there exists "reciprocity, complementarities and interconnectedness" (CSDC 162) in such a way that one cannot be affirmed without affirming the rest, nor can one be denied without denying the rest; and (4) the permanent principles are always the *reference point for the moral guidance and judgments* of Catholic social teaching.

(CSDC 161–163; CCE, *The Religious Dimension of Education in a Catholic School* 1988, 29–42)

95.   Why do these principles have a permanent value?

The fundamental principles of Catholic social teaching have a permanent value because they are an expression of Christian anthropology, that is, an expression of the integral truth of man known by reason and illuminated by faith. They constitute the "primary articulation of the truth of society by which every conscience is challenged" (CSDC 163); they are truths on which the Church has reflected over the centuries, giving them an ever more precise foundation, clarity, and form.

(CSDC 160, 163)

96.   In addition to these fundamental principles, what other principles form part of Catholic social teaching?

The principle of the universal destination of goods and the principle of participation are derived from the permanent principles.

(CSDC 197)

97.   What is the principle of the common good?

As a consequence of the dignity, unity, and equality of all people, the primary goal of every society is the pursuit of the common good, which consists in "the sum total of social conditions which allow people, either as groups or as individuals, to reach their fulfillment more fully and more easily" (CSDC 164, quoting GS 26). Respect for the human person, peace, social well-being, and integral development are all essential elements of the common good. "Just as the moral actions of an individual are accomplished in doing what is good, so too the actions of a society attain their full stature when they bring about the common good. The common good, in fact, can be understood as the social and community dimension of the moral good" (CSDC 164).

(CSDC 164–165; CCC 1907–1909; GS 26)

98. What are the characteristics of the common good?

The common good has five characteristics: (1) it is precisely and above all *common*: only together with every member of society is it possible to attain, increase, and safeguard this good. It is also common because it is the good of all, of each person, and the whole person; and it is therefore not the mere sum of particular goods of each member of society; (2) it is *indivisible*: each member can participate in the common good and it cannot be divided among the members of a society; (3) it always has *the flourishing of all people and of the whole person as its primary goal*; (4) it has a *transcendent dimension*, which extends beyond the present—given that God is the ultimate end of His creatures, the common good cannot be deprived of its transcendent dimension; the common good is not only socioeconomic well-being, but also has a spiritual dimension; and (5) it is an *arduous* good—it is difficult to attain—because "it requires the constant ability and effort to seek the good of others as though it were one's own good" (CSDC 167).

(CSDC 164–165, 167, 170)

99. Who has the responsibility for bringing about the common good?

Because of its characteristics, "the common good therefore involves all members of society, no one is exempt from cooperating, according to each one's possibilities, in attaining it and developing it"[1]

(CSDC 167). In addition to each individual person, the responsibility also belongs to the State, "since the common good is the reason that the political authority exists"[2] (CSDC 168).

(CSDC 167–168; CCC 1908)

100. What are the duties of the political community regarding the common good?

The tasks of the political community are: (1) to guarantee the coherency, unity, and organization of civil society; (2) to work to "make available to persons the necessary material, cultural, moral and spiritual goods" (CSDC 168) so that they may live an authentically human life; (3) to harmonize and reconcile the particular goods and interests of groups and persons, "not only according to the guidelines of the majority but also according to the effective good of all the members of the community, including the minority" (CSDC 169). This is an especially delicate task and corresponds particularly to public authorities.

(CSDC 168–169)

101. What is the principle of the universal destination of goods?

This principle is based on the fact that God created everything that exists and gave the earth to man and woman so that they might have dominion over it with their work and enjoy its fruits (cf. Gn 1:28–29). The principle of the universal destination of goods is at the base of the social ethical order and can be formulated as such: "God destined the earth and all it contains for all men and all peoples so that all created things would be shared fairly by all mankind under the guidance of justice tempered by charity" (CSDC 171, quoting GS 69).

(CSDC 171; GS 69)

102. What are the primary consequences of the principle of the universal destination of goods?

There are two principal consequences: the universal right to the use of goods and the social function of property.

103. What is the universal right to the use of goods?

The human person has a right to "the material goods that corre-spond to his primary needs and constitute the basic conditions for his existence" (CSDC 171). In other words, it is the right to "access to the level of well-being necessary for his full development" (CSDC 172). It is a *natural* right, inscribed in human nature, *inherent*, and has *priority* with regard to any human intervention concerning goods, any legal system governing these goods, and any economic or social system or method.

(CSDC 171–173)

104. What is the social function of property?

The principle of the universal destination of goods also has as a con-sequence the social function of any form of private ownership. The social function of property means that the person "should regard the external things that he legitimately possesses not only as his own but also as common in the sense that they should be able to benefit not only him but also others" (CSDC 178, quoting GS 69). Follow-ing the example of Christ, the social function of property leads us to show special concern for the poor, the marginalized, and those whose life conditions prevent their adequate growth and fulfillment. This is called the *preferential option for the poor.*

(CSDC 178, 182; CCC 2444; MM 19; GS 69)

105. What is meant by the "preferential option for the poor"?

The preferential option for the poor is the Church's love for the poor, "inspired by the Gospel of the Beatitudes, by the poverty of Jesus and by his attention to the poor" (CSDC 184). This love con-cerns both material poverty and the other numerous forms of cul-tural and spiritual poverty present in society today. This special concern for the poor must be translated into a concrete social responsibility; it must make its way into one's way of life and de-cisions, especially those concerning the use of material goods that one possesses.

(CSDC 182–184)

106. Does the universal right to the use of goods mean that private property is unjust?

> No. The principle of the universal destination of goods is not opposed to the right to private property. Private property and other forms of private ownership of goods are absolutely necessary for personal and familial independence and in order to achieve an authentically social and democratic economic policy. However, "Christian tradition has never recognized the right to private property as absolute and untouchable" (CSDC 177), but rather as an instrument at the service of the universal destination of goods, subordinate to it, and with an intrinsic social function.
>
> (CSDC 176–177; LE 14; PP 22–23)

107. How then can private property be reconciled with the universal destination of goods?

> In two ways: first, Catholic social teaching proposes the goal that "all may become, at least in some measure, owners" (CSDC 176); that people, by means of their work, will be able to acquire private property, exercising in this way the universal right to the use of goods. In order to guarantee the ordered and just exercise of the universal right to the use of goods, a *legal order* is necessary—at the national and international levels—that delineates the exercise of this right and regulates rights in property. Just distribution of land deserves special attention, especially in developing countries and those that have recently changed from systems based on collectivization or colonization. Second, private property and the universal destination of goods are reconciled through the moral response of each person and of peoples because "each individual can give and receive" (CSDC 175, quoting LC 90). The social function of property entails an obligation on the part of the owners not to let their goods lay idle and to channel them into productive activity, entrusting them to others who have the desire and the capacity to put them to good use.
>
> (CSDC 175–180)

108. Does the social function of private property also apply to so-called intellectual property?

Yes. Catholic social teaching acknowledges that today more than ever, the practical application of knowledge and technology is becoming more decisive because the wealth of nations increasingly depends on ownership of intellectual property. Thus, in response to the principle of the universal destination of goods, "new technological and scientific knowledge must be placed at the service of mankind's primary needs" (CSDC 179).

(CSDC 179)

109. What is the principle of subsidiarity?

The principle of subsidiarity is founded on human dignity and protects persons' inalienable freedom. In its original formulation, which dates back to the encyclical *Quadragesimo Anno* (cf. QA 78), this principle holds that "a community of a higher order should not interfere in the internal life of a community of a lower order, depriving the latter of its functions, but rather should support it in case of need and help to coordinate its activity with the activities of the rest of society, always with a view to the common good" (CA 48). In a positive sense, subsidiarity is first and foremost a form of assistance to the human person via families and local communities that function autonomously. "Such assistance is offered when individuals or groups are unable to accomplish something on their own, and it is always designed to achieve their emancipation, because it fosters freedom and participation through assumption of responsibility" (CV 57). The word "subsidiarity" comes from the Latin "*subsidium*"—help—and thus refers to an attitude of support, promotion of welfare, and development.
(CSDC 185–186; CA 48; CV 57; QA 78)

110. Is every form of assistance an exercise of subsidiarity?

No. Only those actions that "allow all peoples to become the artisans of their destiny" (PP 65) and to "take up duties of their own" (CV 43) are authentic manifestations of subsidiarity because only assistance that recognizes in the person "a subject who is always capable of giving something to others" (CV 57) is respectful of the person's dignity. The opposite of subsidiarity is the "welfare state," which "by intervening directly and depriving society of its responsibility...

leads to a loss of human energies and an inordinate increase of public agencies, which are dominated more by bureaucratic ways of thinking than by concern for serving their clients, and which are accompanied by an enormous increase in spending" (CA 48).

(CSDC 187; CA 48; CV 43, 57; PP 65)

111. From society's point of view, what is the main purpose of the principle of subsidiarity?

The principle of subsidiarity promotes civil society, understood as the sum of those relationships that form the social fabric and constitute "the basis of a true community of persons, making possible the recognition of higher forms of social activity"[3] (CSDC 185). It is impossible to promote the dignity of the person without showing concern for the family and the various associations that make it possible for people to achieve effective social growth. The principle of subsidiarity guarantees that the expression, capabilities, and initiative of these groups are not destroyed or absorbed into a higher-order social organization.

(CSDC 185; CCC 1882).

112. What are the practical implications of the principle of subsidiarity?

In the first place, subsidiarity seeks to make "citizens more responsible in actively 'being a part' of the political and social reality of their country" (CSDC 187), that is, enabling all people to make their contribution to the common good "because every person, family and intermediate group has something original to offer to the community" (CSDC 187). Consequently, the practical implications of this principle include the "effective promotion of the human person and the family; ever greater appreciation of associations and intermediate organizations…the encouragement of private initiative… safeguarding human rights and the rights of minorities; bringing about bureaucratic and administrative decentralization" (CSDC 187). This must always be done in the framework of the common good, which directs the application of this principle.

(CSDC 187–190)

113. What specific limits does the principle of subsidiarity impose?

The principle of subsidiarity has the goal of avoiding "certain forms of centralization, bureaucratization, and welfare assistance and … the unjustified and excessive presence of the State in public mechanisms.…an absent or insufficient recognition of private initiative—in economic matters also—and the failure to recognize its public function" (CSDC 187). Monopolies that "create delays or obstacles to development" (CSDC 351) are an example of a structure that violates the principle of subsidiarity.

(CSDC 187, 351; CA 48)

114. What special functions belong to the State under the principle of subsidiarity?

In addition to the promotion of the concrete applications of subsidiarity already mentioned, it belongs to the State to step in to supply certain functions in exceptional circumstances, always with a view to the common good. In this sense it belongs to the State to act in situations of "serious social imbalance or injustice where only the intervention of the public authority can create conditions of greater equality, justice and peace" (CSDC 188). It also belongs to the State to promote the economy when it is impossible for civil society to take the initiative. However, "this institutional substitution must not continue any longer than is absolutely necessary" (CSDC 188).

(CSDC 188)

115. What is the principle of participation?

Participation is closely linked to the principle of subsidiarity. It is the first consequence of this principle. It consists in the moral duty of citizens to contribute—individually or in association with others—to the cultural, economic, political, and social life of the community to which they belong. Participation is exercised in distinct and various areas of social life and must be especially promoted among the most disadvantaged.

(CSDC 189; GS 75)

116. What is the importance of participation in community life?

Participation in community life is one of the greatest aspirations of the citizen, one of the pillars of democracy, and one of the best guarantees of the permanence of the democratic system. "Every democracy must be participative.[4] This means that the different subjects of civil community at every level must be informed, listened to and involved in the exercise of the carried-out functions" (CSDC 190).

(CSDC 190)

117. What are the obstacles to participation?

The first obstacle is widespread disinterest in anything concerning social and political life, which causes citizens to "limit their participation to the electoral process, in many cases reaching the point where they even abstain from voting"[5] (CSDC 191). In this respect, "Charges of careerism, idolatry of power, egoism and corruption that are oftentimes directed at persons in government ... as well as the common opinion that participating in politics is an absolute moral danger, does not in the least justify either skepticism or an absence on the part of Christians in public life" (CFL 42). Other obstacles are the various forms of pride that lead citizens to "'make deals' with institutions in order to obtain more advantageous conditions for themselves, as though these institutions were at the service of their selfish needs" (CSDC 191). Lastly, those totalitarian or dictatorial regimes where the fundamental right to participate in public life is denied at its origin, or those where it is only formally recognized but cannot be concretely exercised, are threats to the principle of participation.

(CSDC 191–192; CFL 42; GS 30–31)

118. What is solidarity?

Solidarity is at the same time a principle and a moral virtue. As a *principle*, it indicates that the human person, together with the human family, "is obliged to contribute to the common good of society at all its levels" (LC 73). It is "one of the fundamental principles of the Christian view of social and political organization" (CA 10), and is closely linked to the principles of human dignity, the common good, the universal destination of goods, and subsidiarity. The principle of solidarity also gives rise to the moral *virtue* of solidarity that is "a firm and persevering determination to commit oneself to the common good; that is to say to the good of all and of each individual, because we are all really responsible for all" (SRS 38).

(CSDC 195; CV 58; LC 73; CA 10; SRS 38)

119. What are some of the implications of the principle of solidarity?

"The principle of solidarity requires that men and women of our day cultivate a greater awareness that they are debtors of the society of which they have become part. They are debtors because of those conditions that make human existence livable, and because of the indivisible and indispensable legacy constituted by culture, scientific and technical knowledge, material and immaterial goods and by all that the human condition has produced" (CSDC 195). Likewise, the principle of solidarity particularly calls humanity to address the stark inequalities between developed and developing countries, and those within developed countries. For that reason, solidarity leads people to strive to change the legal structures and economic operations that feed these inequalities.

(CSDC 192–193, 195).

120. What goods does the principle of solidarity protect?

In a context marked by growing interdependence among persons and peoples, the principle of solidarity protects "the equality of all in dignity and rights" (CSDC 192). This principle highlights the link between persons and peoples and is opposed to all forms of individualism and particularism.

(CSDC 192)

121. What is the relation between the principle of solidarity and the principle of subsidiarity in the context of aiding development?

"The principle of subsidiarity must remain closely linked to the principle of solidarity and vice-versa, since the former without the latter gives way to social privatism, while the latter without the former gives way to paternalist social assistance that is demeaning to those in need. This general rule must also be taken broadly into consideration when addressing issues concerning international development aid. Such aid, whatever the donors' intentions, can sometimes lock people into a state of dependence and even foster situations of localized oppression and exploitation in the receiving country" (CV 58).

(CV 58)

122. What is the Christian contribution to the concept of solidarity?

The Christian understanding of solidarity first and foremost offers the example of Jesus Christ who, in becoming man, is the epitome of solidarity with humanity to the point of giving His life on the cross. He demonstrates how Christian solidarity is closely linked to charity. "In the light of faith, solidarity seeks to go beyond itself, to take on the specifically Christian dimension of total gratuity, forgiveness and reconciliation. One's neighbor is then not only a human being with his or her own rights and a fundamental equality with everyone else, but becomes the living image of God.… One's neighbor must therefore be loved, even if an enemy, with the same love with which the Lord loves him or her; and for that person's sake one must be ready for sacrifice, even the ultimate one: to lay down one's life for the brethren (cf. 1 Jn 3:16)" (SRS 40).

(CSDC 196; SRS 40)

123. What are the fundamental values of social life?

The fundamental values of social life are specific aspects of the moral good that the principles of the Church's social teaching aim to achieve. They are "points of reference for the proper structuring and ordered leading of life in society" (CSDC 197). These fundamental values are *truth*, *freedom*, *justice*, and *love*, and they constitute the "indispensable point of reference for public authorities" (CSDC 197).

(CSDC 197)

124. **What is the relationship between the principles and values of Catholic social teaching?**

Principles are the basis from which it is possible to reach the values as goals. There is a relation of mutual interdependence between the two. On the one hand, the principles point toward these values, which are "the sure and necessary way of obtaining personal perfection and a more human social existence" (CSDC 197). On the other hand, achievement of these values requires the practice of the fundamental principles of social life.

(CSDC 197)

125. **What is meant by the value of truth and what is its importance in social life?**

The value of truth means "men and women have the specific duty to move always towards the truth, to respect it and bear responsible witness to it"[6] (CSDC 198). Human coexistence can only be ordered, fruitful, and in conformance with human dignity when it is founded on truth.

(CSDC 198; CCC 2467)

126. **What are the challenges related to the truth faced by society today?**

Today more than ever an intensive educational effort is needed, in addition to a "commitment on the part of all so that the quest for truth cannot be ascribed to the sum of different opinions, nor to one or another of these opinions—will be encouraged in every sector and will prevail over every attempt to relativize its demands or to offend it"[7] (CSDC 198). In society, areas like the economy and public communication make clear the need for and call for a greater transparency and honesty in personal and social activity.

(CSDC 198)

127. **What is the value of freedom?**

Freedom is the greatest sign of the human person being made in the image of God and is thus a sign of his or her sublime dignity. It "consists in the capacity to be in possession of oneself in view of the genuine good, within the context of the universal common good"[8] (CSDC 200). In other words, freedom is the capacity to move oneself toward the good and away from anything that hinders personal, family, or social growth. "It attains its perfection when directed toward God, our beatitude" (CCC 1731).

(CSDC 199–200; CCC 1730–1748)

128. What consequences does the value of freedom have for social life?

Respect for freedom in social life must take form in such a way that each member of society is allowed to fulfill his or her personal vocation. This means that each person must be able to "seek the truth and profess his religious, cultural and political ideas; to express his opinions; to choose his state of life and, as far as possible, his line of work; to pursue initiatives of an economic, social or political nature" (CSDC 200).

(CSDC 199–200)

129. But does freedom focus solely on the individual?

No. A freedom understood as an arbitrary and uncontrolled exercise of one's personal autonomy would be nothing more than selfish individualism. "Freedom only truly exists where reciprocal bonds, governed by truth and justice, link people to one another" (LC 26). Therefore the consequences of freedom for social life identified above "must take place in a 'strong juridical framework,'[9] within the limits imposed by the common good and public order, and, in every case, in a manner characterized by responsibility" (CSDC 200).

(CSDC 199–200; CA 42; LC 26)

130. What is the value of justice?

The value of justice is closely linked to the cardinal virtue of justice, which is "the constant and firm will to give their due to God and neighbor" (CCC 1807). It involves the determination to recognize the other as a person and is also the decisive criterion of morality in the social sphere.

(CSDC 201; CCC 1807)

131. What aspect of justice must be given particular consideration in the present day?

The Magisterium calls for respect for the classic forms of justice: commutative, distributive, and legal or general justice; but, in the present context, special emphasis is given to *social justice*. Social justice obligates society (not just the government) to provide "the conditions that allow associations or individuals to obtain what is their due, according to their nature and their vocation" (CCC 1928). Taking into account the global dimension of social problems, social justice is "a real development in general justice, the justice that regulates social relationships according to the criterion of observance of the law" (CSDC 201). Social justice "concerns the social, political and economic aspects and, above all, the structural dimension of problems and their respective solutions"[10] (CSDC 201).

(CSDC 201; CCC 1928–1933)

132. What are some of the threats to an authentic understanding of justice?

In contemporary society, the importance of justice and the value, dignity, and rights of the human person are constantly voiced; however, what often occurs in reality is that—despite this proclaimed importance—the human person is seriously threatened by the criterion of utility, and one's material possessions are often determinative of one's value. Moreover, there is a widespread "contractualistic" or reductionist vision of justice, where what is just is determined by the law, and is thus a mere human convention. But "what is 'just' is not first determined by the law but by the profound identity of the human being"[11] (CSDC 202).

(CSDC 202–203; SRS 40)

133. What is the role of charity in the structuring of social life?

The Christian vision and human experience demonstrate that "by itself, justice is not enough. Indeed, it can even betray itself, unless it is open to that deeper power which is love"[12] (CSDC 203). Justice is the primary way of charity, its "minimum measure"[13] (CV 6), but justice in turn "must find its fulfillment in charity"[14] (CSDC 206), which is "the highest and universal criterion of the whole of social ethics" (CSDC 204), presupposing and transcending justice. Without charity, "no legislation, no system of rules or negotiation will ever succeed in persuading men and peoples to live in unity, brotherhood and peace; no line of reasoning will ever be able to surpass the appeal of love" (CSDC 207). Consequently, beyond individual action, charity must inform and renew economic and social organizations and legal systems from within.

(CSDC 203–207; CV 6)

5 Life and Love: *The Gospel of the Family*

Jennifer E. Miller

> *Every threat to the family is a threat to society itself. The future of
> humanity, as Saint John Paul II often said, passes through the family....
> So protect your families! See in them your country's greatest treasure
> and nourish them always by prayer and the grace of the sacraments.*
> Pope Francis, Meeting with Families in Manila,
> January 16, 2015

The family is the basic cell or fundamental building block of society; it is the center of social life. Both Church and society have the duty of promoting and fostering the dignity of marriage and family. Families, in turn, are called to actively participate in the mission of the Church and share their gifts with society.

134. Why does the Church speak about the family?

The Church proclaims the good news of Christ to every human person. Since the family is "the first and vital cell of society"[1] (CSDC 211), the place in which the human person learns to live and to love, the Church concerns herself with the family as part of her continuous mission of evangelization to the human person.

(CSDC Preamble to Part II)

135. Why is the family called "the first and vital cell of society"?

The family is the first and vital cell of society because it is the first form of communion between persons, between man and woman. From this communion are born children, who learn in the family and through family interactions what it means to be human and how to live virtuously. This also means that the family is at the center of social life, with rights that belong specifically to this natural society. Both the State and civil society are called to recognize this priority of the family culturally and politically in the face of a contending individualistic mentality.

(CSDC 209–211, 254)

136. How is a family created? What is the relationship between marriage and family?

The family is created through the institution of marriage, which Jesus raised to the level of a sacrament. God, as the author of marriage, has established the meaning of this institution. Marriage is best understood as an irrevocable covenant, as a reciprocal gift of self between husband and wife, which forms a communion of life and love. In this sense, it is very different from a legal contract, where contractual obligations are the primary bonds between two or more people.

(CSDC 212, 215)

137. What does it mean that marriage is a sacrament?

As a sacrament, marriage is an efficacious sign of grace. As a sign, this indissoluble and exclusive covenant until death points to something greater: God's faithful love for His people. This love, seen in salvation history, especially in the Incarnation of God's Son and in the sacrifice of Christ for His Church, is witnessed to by the husband and wife who enter into and live the grace of the Sacrament of Matrimony. The grace of the sacrament assists them both in helping one another to become holy and in working in the life of society so as to bring about the Kingdom of God.

(CSDC 219–220)

138. Is civil law important for marriage?

Civil or State law should be consistent with natural law, which understands that only a man and a woman, in an exclusive and indissoluble relationship, are capable of forming a family, and thus capable of marriage. Since the family is the first and vital cell of society, it falls to all of society to protect and promote families, both for the good of the spouses and children involved as well as for the stability of society, which finds its concrete possibility for existence and growth, at least inasmuch as these arise from procreation, in the family itself. For this reason, divorce and *de facto* unions represent a grave threat to the human person and to the foundations of society. Society, while it can regulate the civil effects of marriage, cannot abolish the right to marriage or change its characteristics.

(CSDC 214, 216, 224–225, 227, 253)

139. How does the Church seek to engage those who have remarried after a divorce?

The Church involves in her life those who have divorced and remarried and encourages them to grow in their faith. The baptized, in this situation, can and must participate in the life of the Church, continue to pray, to raise their children in the faith, and to seek the grace of God. In the Church's fidelity to Christ and to the truth of the Sacrament of Matrimony, the Sacraments of Reconciliation and the Eucharist are open to those who are willing to live a life consistent with the indissolubility of marriage.

(CSDC 226; FC 84)

140. What does the Church say about homosexual unions?

The Church respects the dignity of all persons with homosexual tendencies and encourages them to live a life of chastity. Since the structure of marriage and family is based upon the psychophysical complementarity of a man and woman, and is designed to bear fruit in the children born from their sexual union, the demand for the legal recognition of marriage or of an analogous union between two persons with homosexual tendencies is groundless. Legislation "must never weaken the recognition of indissoluble monogamous marriage as the only authentic form of the family" (CSDC 229).

(CSDC 228–229)

141. Is procreation the only reason for marriage?

Marriage, as a total and permanent gift of self, is meant to bear fruit in the procreation and education of children. However, the irrevocable covenant remains even when husband and wife are unable to conceive. As an unbreakable covenant between two persons, marriage is also directed toward communion, the fostering of mutual love. Furthermore, these couples can become fruitful as well through adoption or through service undertaken for others.

(CSDC 218; GratS 11; GS 50)

142. Does the Church encourage parents to have as many children as possible?

The Church recognizes that the decision concerning when and how many children to bring into the world is one of the inalienable rights of spouses; parents are called to "responsible procreation." The public authorities may never intercede in a way that forces parents to choose between economic assistance and the right to determine how many children they will have. When parents decide—in prayer and in the context of their obligations to their current family and society—to avoid a new birth for a time or even for an indefinite period, periodic abstinence, or natural family planning as it is sometimes called, allows them to do so in terms of mutual respect and total acceptance. However, when sterilization, abortion, and contraception are used, these morally illicit methods undermine the good of the human person and human sexuality.

(CSDC 232–234)

143. Do parents then have a "right to children"?

The desire to have children is a good; however, this desire cannot be realized in such a way that it objectifies children, treating them as products to be acquired. Thus, an absolute "right to children" does not exist; rather, parents must respect the rights of their unborn children. These rights include the right to be born into a stable, loving family founded on marriage as well as the right to be conceived through the love of the conjugal act. For these reasons, parents who desire to have children may use methods that aid the conjugal act, but reproductive technologies that separate this union from conception are unacceptable. Cloning for the purposes of procreation is included within these technologies and is therefore unacceptable.

(CSDC 235–236, 244)

144. Who is responsible for the education of children? What is the role of parents?

Parents are the first and primary educators of their children. Within the loving relationship between parents and children, they educate their children morally and religiously, with a special responsibility for the humanization of sexual education by emphasizing the moral and human values connected with the meaning of sexuality. This is both their right and obligation, which cannot be assumed by anyone else, including the State. However, parents are not the only educators of their children; both the Church and the State are called to aid them in this role.

(CSDC 239–240, 243)

145. How should the State and the family work together?

Since the family is the first and vital cell of society, the relationship between the family and the State should be structured according to the principle of subsidiarity. This means that the family is called not to be a merely passive object of political action but rather to engage the State, local authorities, and family associations actively in forming a society that protects and strengthens the family. The State, when seeking to aid the family, should not attempt to assume its functions but should rather facilitate and sustain the family in accordance with the family's nature as a society. This is true at all economic, social, juridical, and cultural levels.

(CSDC 214, 247; QA 80)

146. How can the State assist parents in educating their children?

Parents have the right to choose the educational institutions that they think will best help them as primary educators. The State and other public authorities are obliged to recognize this right and to ensure the concrete conditions for its exercise. This means that public funds should be available so that parents can support and found the educational institutions of their choice in freedom.

(CSDC 240–241)

147. What is the relationship between the family and the economy?

The family and the market have an important relationship. Within the family, solidarity among generations and the education of children in preparation for their future work make the economy possible. On the other hand, the right of a person to adequate compensation for work is the essential condition for beginning and maintaining a family. For this reason, the Church insists upon a "just wage," which can be better understood as a "family wage."

(CSDC 248–249; LE 19; QA 70–75; VBL 77)

148. What is a "family wage"?

A family wage allows a family to live decently and to save in order to buy property that can secure future economic stability. Social provisions to aid in bringing about this wage can take several forms: family subsidies, compensation for domestic work done in the home, and contributions for dependent family members. In this context, more emphasis and greater value should be put on the work done by women in the home.

(CSDC 250–251; LE 19)

149. What concrete gifts does the family offer to an individualistic society?

In a society that often focuses on the efficiency and functionality of the individual ("cost-efficiency," as it is sometimes called), the family springs from the concrete choice for love and gratuitousness between a man and woman. It accepts and values those who would be left out of a cost-efficient society, those who are incapable of producing, such as the elderly, the sick, and children. It prizes above all the importance of human, cultural, and moral values in interpersonal relationships and lives a love that is faithfulness.

(CSDC 221–223, 246; FC 43)

Special Topic: *Gender Theory*

Antonio Malo

150. What is gender theory?

Gender theory is a school of thought that, in its attempt to bring about "self-emancipation from creation and the Creator" (Benedict XVI, *Christmas Address to the Roman Curia* 2008, 1), aims to advance a libertarian or "free" approach to issues related to sexuality, marriage, and family. The distinction between sex and gender is a central element of this theory, which emerged in feminist circles in North America in the late 1960s and 1970s and has since spread throughout much of the world.

151. How does gender theory define the terms sex and gender?

With the term "sex," gender theory means that which is *given* in nature, that is, one's biological makeup or bodily sex. The term "gender," on the other hand, is understood as a social construct that defines the roles of men and women; and, being cultural, these are necessarily subject to change. In its most radical forms, gender theory states that everyone should be able to choose his or her gender, independent of his or her own body and existing conjugal and family ties.

152. What are the positive aspects of gender theory?

Gender theory emphasizes the personal nature of human sexuality. The scientific analysis of this reality reveals that human sexuality, in addition to being rooted in the body, must also be personalized through psychological identification with one's own sex and through appropriate interpersonal relations, beginning with one's relationship with his or her parents. Additionally, gender theory rightly points out that some of the social roles attributed to men and women throughout history are merely conventional and have negatively impacted how society values women.

153. How does gender theory differ from the Church's understanding of human sexuality?

Pope Francis stated, "I ask myself, if the so-called gender theory is not … an expression of frustration and resignation, which seeks to cancel out sexual difference because it no longer knows how to confront it" (Francis, *General Audience* April 15, 2015). While the Church proclaims the *equal dignity* of man and woman, she also celebrates their *differences*. In ignoring the sexual difference, in seeing it as something that can (and should) be overcome, gender theory loses the *originality* of femininity and masculinity. "Womanhood expresses the 'human' as much as manhood does, but in a different and complementary way" (LW 7). One's sex is not simply a matter of biology. "Sexuality characterizes man and woman not only on the physical level, but also on the psychological and spiritual, making its mark on each of their expressions" (CCE, *Educational Guidance in Human Love* 1983, 5).

154. On what points does gender theory contradict the Bible?

The two creation accounts definitively confirm the importance of the sexual difference. In the first account we are told that "God created mankind in his image; / in the image of God he created them; / male and female he created them" (Gn 1:27). In the second account, man realizes that he is alone and God makes Adam "a helper suited to him" (Gn 2:18). This help is mutual and does not imply any kind of inferiority of women to men. This help does not just refer to actions, but to the *being* of men and women. Man and woman are complementary not only on a physical level, but in their very existence. They complete one another; the man offers the woman something only he can give and the woman offers the man something only she can give.

(MW 6; LW 7)

155. On what points does gender theory contradict morality?

Gender theory also contradicts sexual morality. First, in making a radical distinction between sex and gender, it denies both the procreative and the unitive meanings of human sexuality, as can be seen in its attitude toward homosexual relations, in which there is not true communion due to an absence of the sexual difference. Second, based on this separation between sex and gender, gender theorists claim that homosexual relationships are capable of constituting a marriage. However, despite the deep feelings and commitment that may be present in these relationships, they are not marriage because they lack the sexual difference, and thus cannot be the origin of a family.

(CSDC 229; LF 52; EG 66)

156. What kind of effect does gender theory have on society?

Gender theory affects society on two levels. On the political and legislative level, gender theorists pressure for change in the physiognomy of marriage and family. They call for the legalization and social acceptance of new models of marriage and family in the name of progress, tolerance, and equal rights, including the right to adopt children. This so-called "progress," however, will only contribute to the self-destruction of the human person and society (cf. Benedict XVI, *Christmas Address to the Roman Curia* 2008). On the cultural level, gender theory seeks to change the governing mentalities, beginning with those most vulnerable to indoctrination: children and adolescents. Under the guise of educating them in tolerance, they are encouraged to "explore" and "experiment" with their sexuality so that they can choose that which best suits them.

157. Why does the Church denounce gender theory as an ideology?

The Church, which has always been interested in that which concerns man and woman, denounces gender theory as an ideology because she has the right and the duty to intervene when the natural and supernatural good of persons and society are at stake. She has received from God a "responsibility for creation" (Benedict XVI, *Christmas Address to the Roman Curia* 2008, 4). For this reason, the Church promotes a "human ecology" that helps nations and States to differentiate between that which constitutes true progress and that which is instead a step back, resulting in the disintegration of people and the social fabric.

(Benedict XVI, *Christmas Address to the Roman Curia* 2008)

158. What is this "human ecology" that the Church promotes?

In her responsibility towards creation, the Church must first and foremost protect mankind, which forms part of creation. Human ecology means respect for the human person and "the natural and moral structure with which he has been endowed" (CA 38). This includes the promotion of the values of femininity and masculinity as the foundation of the humanization of persons. "Every outlook which presents itself as a conflict between the sexes is only an illusion and a danger: it would end in segregation and competition between men and women" (MW 14).

On a more concrete level, human ecology applies to social policies concerning education, family, work, access to services, civic participation, and so on. On the one hand, we must combat any unjust sexual discrimination. On the other hand, and at the same time, the promotion of equal dignity "must be harmonized with attentive recognition of the difference and reciprocity between the sexes where this is relevant to the realization of one's humanity, whether male or female" (MW 14; cf. CCC 2358).

(CA 38–39; CV 51)

159. Gender theory has been referred to as an "ideological colonization." What does this mean?

Gender theory has been called an ideological colonization because it attempts, using every means at its disposal, to impose a vision of sexuality, marriage, and family that is inhuman, and therefore capable of enslaving people (cf. Francis, *In-flight Press Conference from the Phillipines to Rome* January 19, 2015). Gender theory seeks to mask this manipulation. It claims to offer greater freedom, when in reality it is its denial. It claims to help each person discover his or her sexual identity, when in reality it prevents man and woman from recognizing and accepting his or her sexual identity. It fails to recognize that the physical, moral, and spiritual *difference* and *complementarity* between man and woman are directed towards the goods of celibacy or marriage and the development of family life.

(CCC 2333)

160. **What should Christians do to counteract the negative influence of gender theory?**

This task begins in the home. Christians should actively participate in the education of their children, because through it the Christian culture is passed on and progresses from generation to generation. Furthermore, the family environment has to be such that children learn to love in being freely loved, to respect others in being respected, and to know the face of God firstly through a father and mother who are attentive to them. This way, daughters and sons discover the beauty of maternity and paternity and therefore of the femininity and masculinity that they respectively embody. When these fundamental experiences are absent or lacking, there is a loss of humanity in society; society as a whole suffers and in turn becomes a creator of violence.

(CSDC 242–243; MW 13–14; CCE, *Educational Guidance in Human Love* 1983)

6 Human Work, Labor, and Workers' Rights

MARTIN SCHLAG

The basis for determining the value of human work is not primarily the kind of work being done but the fact that the one who is doing it is a person.

POPE JOHN PAUL II, *LABOREM EXERCENS*, 6

Work is part of God's original plan and even constitutes a path to holiness. However, for many, work has long been a source of oppression rather than fulfillment. The plight of workers, their misery and suffering, was the reason behind the first social encyclical in 1891. Since then a lot of progress has been made, but much still needs to be done at home and abroad. The Church continues to proclaim the rights of the working man and woman.

161. Is work part of God's original plan or a punishment for original sin?

Work is not a punishment for sin. The hardships, exhaustion, and frustrations that sometimes accompany work are. Prior to original sin, however, God invited man to work the soil and cultivate and care for the garden in which he had been placed. All of creation is good, and was created for the good of mankind. Work is part of this goodness, and God wants us to cooperate through our work in the creation that He began.

(CSDC 255, 262; Gn 2:15)

162. How is it that men and women cooperate with God's creation when they work?

God the Father has ordered the universe through His Wisdom (Jesus) and Love (the Holy Spirit). Through their work, men and women share in this divine love and wisdom, and unfold God's plan for creation. By transforming matter into goods that serve other people, we put God's creation to the service of mankind as He wishes. Working side by side with others we increase the common good, above all to the benefit of those in need.

(CSDC 262–263, 266, 275)

163. What did Jesus teach about work?

Jesus taught us about work first and foremost by His example. He is a man of work and teaches us to appreciate work. Jesus Himself devoted many years of His life on earth to manual work as a carpenter; and during His public ministry He worked tirelessly, performing miracles and freeing people from sickness, suffering, and death.

(CSDC 259–261)

164. Jesus told His followers not to worry about food and clothing. Isn't working for these things contrary to His teaching?

Jesus does not say that we do not need these things, nor that we shouldn't work or care for them. He wants us to trust in God and not to be enslaved by fear. Work should not be a source of anxiety. When people are worried and upset about many things, they run the risk of neglecting the Kingdom of God and His righteousness (cf. Mt 6:33).

(CSDC 260)

165. What does Christianity say about work? Is it good in itself or is it a sort of necessary burden, an obstacle to the leisure that allows us time for higher pursuits like family, prayer, and culture?

Christian faith honors work and considers it to be a human duty. No Christian who is capable of working has the right not to work, taking advantage of and living off of the charity of others (cf. 2 Thes 3:6–12). "Rather, all are charged by the Apostle Paul to make it a point of honor to work with their own hands, so as to 'be dependent on nobody' (1 Thes 4:12), and to practice a solidarity which is also material by sharing the fruits of their labor with 'those in need' (Eph 4:28)" (CSDC 264).

(CSDC 264–265, 274)

166. But isn't the problem today that people work too much and have no time for other things?

This can sometimes be the case. Work is an important part of our life, but not its only purpose. Work must not become an idol because the ultimate and definitive meaning of life is not to be found in work. Only God is the origin of life and the final goal of man.

(CSDC 257)

167. Why is it important to rest on Sunday and on the other feast days?

The Bible tells us that God rested on the seventh day of creation, the Sabbath. Without this rest, God's work would not have been complete. The Sabbath is a barrier against becoming slaves to work, and especially serves to protect the poor against exploitation. It ensures that human work does not destroy the relationships and communities in which we live.

(CSDC 258)

168. What exactly is "rest"? What should Christians do on Sunday?

On Sundays and holy days of obligation, Catholics are to attend Mass (cf. CCC 2042). And, on these days, believers must "refrain from engaging in work or activities that hinder the worship owed to God, the joy proper to the Lord's Day, the performance of the works of mercy, and the appropriate relaxation of mind and body"[1] (CCC 2185).

(CSDC 284–285)

169. Can normal professional work be a vocation to holiness and evangelization?

When we unite our work with Christ's redemption, then "work can be considered a means of sanctification and an enlivening of earthly realities with the Spirit of Christ"[2] (CSDC 263).

(CSDC 263)

170. Is a life of hard work compatible with intense prayer?

Yes. When it is directed towards charity as its final goal, human work becomes an occasion for contemplation and devout prayer. This gives work a spiritual dimension.

(CSDC 266)

171. Why does the Church deal with work in her social teaching?

Since the encyclical *Rerum Novarum*, the Church has dealt with work in connection with the "worker question," that is, the problem of the exploitation of workers. In her social teaching, the Church defends the inalienable dignity of workers, and has never stopped considering the problems of workers within the context of the social question, which has progressively taken on worldwide dimensions.

(CSDC 267–269)

172. Is a person defined by his or her work? Does one's dignity stem from his or her occupation?

No, human dignity comes from being made in the image and likeness of God. That is why John Paul II distinguished between the subjective and objective dimensions of work. The objective dimension of work consists in the output, the tools and machines, and the exterior circumstances of work. The subjective dimension refers to the worker as an acting person. The two dimensions are connected, but the subjective dimension is more important. It is in his subjective dimension as a person that the worker possesses dignity. In other words, it is the worker—the person—that confers dignity on his or her work, and not the other way around.

(CSDC 270–271)

173. A person's dignity may not stem from his or her work, but can't work sometimes violate a person's dignity?

Yes. Whenever a worker is viewed as a simple commodity or an impersonal cogwheel in a machine, his or her dignity is violated. Work is for man, not man for work. This has consequences for the relationship of work to capital, for the right to work, and for one's rights in work.

(CSDC 271–272)

174. What is the relationship between work and capital?

"Capital" refers to the material items used for production in a given enterprise (farmland, tools, factories, machines, etc.), and the financial resources (money, credit, shares, bonds, etc.) employed to bring about production or used in financial markets. Work, because of its subjective or personal character, is superior to capital. However, they are interdependent. You cannot have one without the other: capital without human work is useless; work without capital is ineffective. For example, a machine without anyone working at it is useless, just as many people trying to work without tools is ineffective.

(CSDC 276–277)

175. That sounds easier than seems to be the case in real life. Haven't there been tensions between labor and capital?

Yes. Work and capital have often been in conflict in the past, and those tensions tend to resurface when the socioeconomic circumstances change. There is a risk that capital will exploit and alienate workers. People are alienated when more importance is placed on profits than on their dignity. Finding the correct relationship between work and capital so as to guarantee the worker's dignity is a continuous challenge.

(CSDC 279–280)

176. What other aspects must be taken into consideration regarding the relationship between work and capital?

Work entails the right to participate in the life of the company in which one works. The specific forms of participation depend on the circumstances of each society, and vary according to the different concrete situations.

(CSDC 281)

177. Are there special aspects of the dignity of work in agriculture?

Agriculture is very important for mankind because it produces our daily food. Unfortunately, in some countries an unproductive system of immense landholdings that are not being farmed (*latifundium*) is in place. In these cases, a redistribution of land as part of agrarian reform is desirable in order to achieve genuine economic development.

(CSDC 299–300; LS 124–129)

178. Does the mining or extractive industry have any special ethical responsibilities?

Yes. Mining is an important industry that makes the earth's natural resources available for the needs of mankind. However, not infrequently mining companies from rich countries extract minerals and natural resources in poor developing countries, sometimes with the complicity of those in power in the poor countries, to "ensure their own prosperity at the expense of the well-being of the local population" (AM 79). The Church must speak out against the unjust order that prevents the poor from consolidating their economies. Moreover, everywhere in the world, mining can destroy farmland, pollute the environment, and cause desertification. Serious damage is thus done to the economic foundation of populations that are not prepared for or are unable to adapt to unprecedented changes to their lifestyle and means of sustenance.

(AM 79–80)

179. Why does the Church uphold the "right to work"?

The Church upholds the "right to work" because work is a good for mankind that enables men and women to give expression to and enhance their human dignity. Besides, work is necessary in order to earn one's livelihood and that of the family. Work does not just refer to labor for wages, but also includes any serious effort to serve other people's needs in a systematic way; therefore parenting, managing a household, voluntary work, and so on are also work. For most people, however, work is performed for income, and is necessary to form and maintain a family, to acquire property, and to contribute to the common good of society.

(CSDC 287)

180. What does the Church say about unemployment?

Unemployment is a "real social disaster" (CSDC 287, quoting LE 18), especially when it afflicts the younger generations. Full employment is therefore an important objective for every society that is oriented toward justice and the common good.

(CSDC 287–288)

181. What should a national government do to make work available to all who are capable of engaging in it?

Governments should encourage the creation of employment opportunities within their national territories. This duty does not consist of directly guaranteeing work for every citizen, because this would make economic life rigid and restrict free, individual initiative, but in creating conditions that permit economic growth and ensure integral human development.

(CSDC 291)

182. What can the international community do to promote full employment?

In the globalized economy work has become mobile: firms move to countries where work is cheaper and where there are fewer restrictions regarding the treatment of workers. The family of nations should promote international cooperation in order to protect workers' rights, especially with regard to safety at work and proper wages.

(CSDC 292)

183. Can't the necessity of working to maintain one's livelihood collide with the other duties we have to our family?

Yes, this can indeed happen. The family needs work for its material livelihood but it also needs time together. It is not easy to implement policies that do not penalize but rather support the family nucleus. However, it is a challenge worth taking up: family life and work mutually affect one another in many ways.

(CSDC 294)

184. Does the right to work also apply to women?

Yes. Men and women are created equal in dignity and rights, and this is also true with respect to pay, insurance, and social security. However, the *functions* of men and women are not identical. The "feminine genius" can contribute something unique in all expressions of social life; the presence of women in the workplace is thus very important. Additionally, the organization of work should not be an obstacle to the unique role of women in the family.

(CSDC 295; LW 9–12)

185. What does the Church say about child labor?

There are societies and cultures in which children work for their families according to their age and capabilities. If no damage is caused to their health, and there is sufficient time left for education and play, then this kind of work is a contribution to the family economy and is not a violation of human dignity. However, any harmful form of child labor is intolerable and constitutes a kind of violence.

(CSDC 296)

186. Do immigrants have a right to work?

Yes. Every human person possesses the right to work. The great inequalities that exist between poor and rich countries lead a growing number of people to seek work in other places in order to sustain their families. This pressure is the reason why immigration must be regulated by law, according to the criteria of justice and mercy. This means that the Church does not promote an open border policy; however, there is a right to move to another country rather than starve in one's own. Even though people who enter a country in violation of the laws are undocumented immigrants, they are to be treated as persons with human dignity, which means they also have the moral right to work.

(CSDC 297–298)

187. What are the rights of workers once they are employed?

Workers who have found employment possess the rights that stem from their dignity as human persons. Some of these rights are the right to a just wage; the right to rest; the right "to a working environment and to manufacturing processes which are not harmful to the workers' physical health or to their moral integrity" (CSDC 301, quoting LE 19); the right to social security connected with unemployment, old age, illness, and maternity; and the right to assemble and form associations.

(CSDC 301)

188. What qualifies as a just wage?

Generally speaking, a wage is just if it corresponds to the value that the work adds to the company's productivity. The just wage is the fruit of one's work that permits the laborer to provide for his or her livelihood and to become an owner of private property, which is an important means of gaining independence. Employers who refuse to pay a just wage or who do not give it in due time and in proportion to the work done commit grave injustice (cf. Lv 19:13; Dt 24:14–15; Jas 5:4). Employers should do their best to guarantee the well-being of their workers and their families.

(CSDC 302)

189. Is the economic well-being of a country measured exclusively by the quantity of goods it produces?

No, it should not only be measured by the quantity of material goods but also by the manner in which they are produced and the level of equity in the country's distribution of income. Therefore an economy does not function well if wages are unjust, if opportunities are unfair, or if the playing field for competition is not level.

(CSDC 303)

190. What does the Church say about unions?

The specific task of unions is to secure the just rights of workers within the framework of the common good of the whole of society. The Church recognizes this fundamental role played by labor unions as a form of solidarity among workers. The Church also teaches that relations within the world of work should be marked by cooperation. Strikes are sometimes inevitable as a last resort; however, hatred and attempts to abuse or eliminate the other in violent forms of class struggle are unacceptable.

(CSDC 304–307)

191. The world of work is in constant evolution and change. What does this mean for the social teaching of the Church on work?

The historical forms change, but not the permanent requirements of the inalienable human rights of workers. Changes, like those caused by globalization and technological progress, bring about economic and social imbalances. These must be addressed by restoring a just hierarchy of values, and by placing the human dignity of workers before all else. This is the never-ending challenge of Christian humanism in the areas of business, work, and society on a global scale.

(CSDC 319, 321–322)

Special Topic: *Immigration*

ELIZABETH REICHERT

192. Do people have a right to migrate?

All people have a right to secure the basic necessities of life. "When there are just reasons in favor for it, [one] must be permitted to emigrate to other countries and take up residence there. The fact that he is a citizen of a particular State does not deprive him of membership to the human family, nor of citizenship in that universal society, the common, world-wide fellowship of men" (PT 25).

(PT 25)

193. What are the rights and duties of unauthorized or undocumented immigrants?

Undocumented immigrants are especially vulnerable to exploitation, and are sometimes seen as undeserving of rights and human services. A person's legal status does not strip him or her of dignity. "Every migrant is a human person who, as such, possesses fundamental, inalienable rights that must be respected by everyone and in every circumstance" (CV 62). Along with these rights come corresponding duties: "Immigrants are obliged to respect with gratitude the material and spiritual heritage of the country that receives them, to obey its laws and to assist in carrying civic burdens" (CCC 2241).

(CSDC 297–298; CCC 2241; CV 62)

194. Won't immigrants steal jobs from legal citizens and be a burden on the State?

"Immigration can be a resource for development rather than an obstacle to it....These people come from less privileged areas of the earth and their arrival in developed countries is often perceived as a threat to the high levels of well-being achieved thanks to decades of economic growth. In most cases, however, immigrants fill a labor need which would otherwise remain unfilled in sectors and territories where the local workforce is insufficient or unwilling to engage in the work in question" (CSDC 297). They make a contribution both to the local economy through their labor, purchases, and taxes, and to their home country by sending money to their families. At the same time, they "cannot be considered as a commodity or a mere workforce" (CV 62); each immigrant—documented or not—is a human person, and as such possesses a fundamental dignity and inalienable rights.

(CSDC 297–298; CV 62; GS 66)

195. What are the government's primary duties concerning immigration?

The Church proclaims that when there are just reasons people have the right to migrate. Thus, "the more prosperous nations are obliged, to the extent they are able, to welcome the *foreigner*" (CCC 2241). At the same time, the Church does not promote an "open borders" policy. Governments have both the right and the duty to secure their borders and enforce their laws. "No country can be expected to address today's problems of migration by itself" (CV 62).

These apparently conflicting rights and duties are reconciled by a third principle: a country must regulate its borders with justice and mercy, or with "equity and balance"[1] (CSDC 298). "A nation may not simply decide that it wants to provide for its own people and no others. A sincere commitment to the needs of all must prevail" (USCCB, *Catholic Social Teaching on Immigration and the Movement of Peoples*).

(CSDC 298; CCC 2241; CV 62)

196. What are some positive steps that can be taken in immigration reform?

We cannot turn a blind eye to the suffering of our sisters and brothers and the thousands who have left behind house and home only to lose their lives crossing deserts or treacherous waters in the hopes of a brighter future. "This is a striking phenomenon because of the sheer numbers of people involved, the social, economic, political, cultural and religious problems it raises, and the dramatic challenges it poses to nations and the international community. We can say that we are facing a social phenomenon of epoch-making proportions that requires bold, forward-looking policies of international cooperation if it is to be handled effectively" (CV 62).

We must first address the root causes of migration (e.g., combating poverty by promoting sustainable economic development). Second, legal systems regarding immigration are in need of reform. The Church does not advocate illegal immigration, but she does advocate changing a broken system. Practical steps include offering paths for legal immigration, reuniting families, and offering earned legalization for undocumented immigrants.

(CSDC 298; CV 62; USCCB, *Frequently Asked Questions About Comprehensive Immigration Reform*)

7 Economic Life: *Development, Prosperity, and Justice for All*

MARTIN SCHLAG

> *We cannot separate what we believe from how we act in the marketplace and the broader community, for this is where we make our primary contribution to the pursuit of economic justice.*
> USCCB, ECONOMIC JUSTICE FOR ALL, 25

The Church not only urges us to have a heart for the poor, but she also emphasizes the importance of having a *mind* for the poor. Those who work in business and economics can be such "a mind." Business, if it obeys legal and moral laws, does a lot of good. Businesses create jobs, produce goods, make innovations, and improve our lives. The Church wants an economy that produces wealth, prosperity, and justice for all, not just a few.

197. What do we mean by "economy"?

Economy is the effort to meet the material needs of the human person in a safe and sustainable way. Concretely, this includes the production, distribution, and consumption of goods and services. These factors enable the survival and the development of individuals, societies, and the world.

198. What is the goal of the economy?

The goal of the economy is to make available the goods and services that all human beings need for their survival and to enable the development that God desires for them. The resources to do this (raw materials, machinery, land, labor, etc.) are scarce. We therefore need to organize the economy and create systems in which these scarce materials are used as efficiently as possible. The origin and the end of the entire economy is the human person. As in all other human activities, in economic life human dignity must be respected and promoted, as must be the person's vocation to development and the common good of society as a whole.

(CSDC 334, 346, 375; GS 63)

199. What is the relationship between economy and ethics?

As in every sphere of social life, the economy has its own logic and laws. Our economic system is the market economy, in which the market is the most important institution. In this "space" of the market (like eBay, for example), many buyers and sellers meet to negotiate freely over price, quantity, and quality of products.

The market economy is highly efficient, but to be truly free and good, it needs virtues, ethical norms, a culture of work, and clear legal rules guaranteed by the State. It must also provide for those who cannot offer anything to the market, for example, those unable to work because of illness or age or those who are penniless through no fault of their own. The Second Vatican Council has explicitly recognized the legitimate "autonomy of earthly realities," but stressed that it is not "absolute," but simply "relative" (cf. GS 36). The laws of the market are subject to divine laws and cannot justify immoral behavior. Furthermore, ethics is an essential part of good governance and management. This means that unethical actions—in the long run—are also *economically* erroneous, and vice-versa: economically erroneous actions are *immoral* because they lead to a waste of resources.

(CSDC 330–333; GS 36)

200. What does this mean in practice?

An increase of wealth is morally good if it is not only for a few, but rather improves the situation of all people. Development cannot be limited solely to an increase in consumption or economic growth, but should include the integral development of the whole person. Furthermore, an increase in consumption without the knowledge of how to sustain and reproduce this increase, is not true development.

Faith, family, education, health, and many other values are included in the concept of development. Seeking happiness only in consumption is actually a form of moral poverty ("consumerism"). Therefore, good business must account also for the development of the whole person, rather than just one aspect of his or her well-being—albeit an important one—that of his or her consumption.

(CSDC 334)

201. What is the Church's general attitude to the economy?

The Church views the economy in a positive light. She wants the poor to be structurally included in the economy, so that ever-increasing numbers of people will have the dignity of earning their own livelihood, and be able to enjoy at least a modest prosperity, living without fear of poverty.

(CSDC 373–374; GS 63, 65; EG 202)

202. What is globalization?

The global economy is increasingly interconnected and interdependent. Globalization is a process that began with the decreased importance of national borders in economic relations after the Cold War. It was made possible by the improvement of transportation infrastructures and the digital revolution, which led to the transfer of production to places where it could be performed more cheaply, the opening of new markets, and freer sources of finance. Furthermore, world travel has become much easier, information can be freely exchanged, etc.

(CSDC 361)

203. What does the Church say about globalization?

Globalization is an encouraging process for the international community, offering hope for a brighter and more sustainable economic future, but it also raises causes for concern. The hope comes from the development and improvement of the material and cultural conditions of life on a global scale. The concerns stem from an increased inequality, exploitation of the poor, and the loss of cultural identity. In an era of globalization, solidarity among peoples and among generations becomes especially important.

(CSDC 342, 362–367)

204. How can development be promoted?

Development cannot be equated solely with economic growth. To achieve development—in addition to economic growth—the participation of certain institutions is required: first the family, then education and medical care, among others. One of the tasks of the international economy is to achieve an integral and coherent development for all of humanity, that is, for every person and for the whole person. It is not true that the rich necessarily become richer while the poor become poorer. In an economic system worthy of human dignity, economic prosperity for one group improves conditions for everyone. Development within the poor countries is for this reason advantageous for the richer countries too.

(CSDC 373–374)

205. Can business be a vocation?

Yes. God calls everyone to holiness in a special and personal way. "Business is a noble vocation, directed to producing wealth and improving our world. It can be a fruitful source of prosperity for the areas in which it operates, especially if it sees the creation of jobs as an essential part of its service to the common good" (LS 129). It is a matter of justice to use well the gifts one has received, including material gifts. Jesus praises this attitude in the parable of the talents (cf. Mt 25:14–30; Lk 19:11–27).

(CSDC 326; LS 129)

206. Jesus was poor. How then can one follow Christ in business?

Christians are called to put into practice and to disseminate the virtues of faith, hope, and love—even in the business world. Anyone who follows Jesus must remember the obligation to become "rich in what matters to God" (Lk 12:21). The most important goal in life cannot be to accumulate material riches; it is, rather, to love God above all else, and to contribute with love to the development of people and society. Depending on a man or woman's individual calling, one way of doing this can be through a vocation to business.

(CSDC 326)

207. What does the Bible say about wealth and poverty?

The Bible says we should not aspire to riches for their own sake, but to those goods that make possible a happy life. Money must never become an idol. Jesus teaches us to pray: "Give us this day our daily bread." With these words we ask the Father for what is necessary for our earthly life. We pray for the sustenance of our family, but also for the poor and for all men and women in the world.

(CSDC 323–325)

208. Is poverty always bad?

When poverty is involuntary and involves misery and the lack of basic resources, then it is always an evil. "The poverty of the world is a scandal. In a world where there is such great wealth, so many resources for giving food to everyone, it is impossible to understand how there could be so many hungry children, so many children without education, so many poor people!" (Francis, *Address to the Students of the Jesuit Schools of Italy and Albania* 2013).

However, a situation of relative poverty that does not threaten human dignity can lead people to recognize their true needs before God, leading them to turn to Him and trust Him for their needs. While all who want to follow Jesus must be "poor in spirit" (Mt 5:3), there are those who voluntarily renounce wealth in order to serve God with a free heart. The men and women who live in this way bear witness to the world of our calling to love God above all things.

(CSDC 324; EG 53)

209. Is prosperity always good?

A certain measure of prosperity is good because we can dedicate time to friendship, culture, and religion. However, there are the dangers of arrogance, presumption, and insensitivity to others. A rich person might think his well-being is only the result of his own efforts apart from God. Jesus warned against such pride: "You fool, this night your life will be demanded of you; and the things you have prepared, to whom will they belong?" (Lk 12:20).

(CSDC 325)

210. How can we understand the words of Jesus: "Do not worry about tomorrow; tomorrow will take care of itself" (Mt 6:34)—is this not a contradiction of the economic way of thinking?

No. Providing prudently for one's self and for others is consistent with the words of Jesus; Jesus also lived with such an attitude as a craftsman who worked for others. Anxiety for the future, on the other hand, is incompatible with the trust of a child of God.

(CCC 523)

211. How should a Christian respond to his or her own poverty?

A Christian should do everything morally possible to free himself and his family from poverty through patient and diligent work. Sometimes, together with others, he will also have to overcome structures of exclusion that hinder the progress of the poor.

(CSDC 325)

212. How should a Christian respond to the poverty of others?

A Christian shares in the joy and the pain of others because we are all sisters and brothers. We must make every effort to not only show compassion, but also to alleviate the suffering of others as we are able. The specific ways of achieving this task will differ greatly for each person. In general, there are two ways of approaching poverty. First, one can help the poor directly through donations. While this is necessary in order to meet the immediate needs of those in desperate situations, we must also work together with the poor to find long-term solutions. This is the second approach. Such solutions will enable the poor to free themselves from poverty; for example, by helping them find work and providing job training and affordable education. Entrepreneurs make an important contribution to reducing poverty by creating jobs and dignified working conditions. Even though needs are immense, no one ought to feel overwhelmed by and thus exempt from the works of mercy.

(CSDC 329; CCC 2447)

213. Are the Kingdom of God and earthly progress the same thing?

Jesus said, "My kingdom does not belong to this world" (Jn 18:36). The Kingdom of God should not be confused with material or earthly progress. However, "to the extent that [earthly progress] can contribute to the better ordering of human society, it is of vital concern to the Kingdom of God" (GS 39). The awareness of our responsibility before God to the world is a great incentive to work for integral development.

(CSDC 55; GS 39)

214. Does the Catholic Church identify with a specific economic model such as socialism, capitalism, or liberalism?

In general terms, the Church favors a market economy that includes every person and all peoples, and is guided by the principles of social justice and charity. The Church, however, does not identify herself with any specific economic model or political party. She does not propose "technical solutions"; she proposes the gospel. Over the centuries, drawing from the gospel, some principles for social life have been elaborated, such as the respect for human dignity, solidarity, and subsidiarity. Christians active in the economic sector are called to apply these principles according to a well-formed conscience.

(CSDC 72)

215. So the Church never intervenes on questions of economic detail?

If the fundamental rights of the person or the salvation of souls require it, the Church must raise her voice to denounce social injustices and abuses.

(GS 76; CCC 2245–2246)

216. What does the Church say about capitalism?

With the failure of central planning in the Soviet system in mind, John Paul II addressed the question of whether countries should adopt capitalism: "If by 'capitalism' is meant an economic system which recognizes the fundamental and positive role of business, the market, private property and the resulting responsibility for the means of production, as well as free human creativity in the economic sector, then the answer is certainly in the affirmative, even though it would perhaps be more appropriate to speak of a 'business economy', 'market economy' or simply 'free economy'. But if by 'capitalism' is meant a system in which freedom in the economic sector is not circumscribed within a strong juridical framework which places it at the service of human freedom in its totality, and which sees it as a particular aspect of that freedom, the core of which is ethical and religious, then the reply is certainly negative" (CA 42).

(CSDC 335; CA 42)

217. How must the economic order be changed in order to effectively serve the human person and the common good?

Every social change begins with the individual, with his or her own internal renewal. However, the community also has the duty to improve its social institutions and structures. To achieve this goal, a combination of personal virtues and social and economic institutions is needed. The necessary economic institutions will be characterized by, among other things, private property, money, profit, and competition in the free market. The necessary social institutions will include the political community to which one belongs. Among the virtues, justice and love are of particular importance. These virtues lead each person to work honestly and transparently, and they also motivate the person to perform volunteer and non-profit work.

(CSDC 42, 343–345; CCC 1888)

218. What does the Church say about private property?

Everyone has a natural right to the fruits of his labor and the means to achieve these fruits. In the case of large expanses of unproductive land, and of people eager to till it, there is "a natural right to possess a reasonable allotment of land where [persons] can establish [their] home, work for subsistence of [their] family and a secure life. This right must be guaranteed so that its exercise is not illusory but real. That means that apart from the ownership of property, rural people must have access to means of technical education, credit, insurance, and markets"[1] (LS 94).

(CSDC 176–184, GS 71; LS 94)

219. Is this an absolute right?

This right to private property creates individual freedom by granting material independence, promotes hard work, and clarifies what belongs to whom, thereby contributing to shared prosperity and social peace. However, the grave inequalities that can result are a cause of tension and injustice. The economic superiority of one person may put the other in a position of inferiority and disadvantage. This can lead to exploitation in work relations or economic relations in general. For this reason it is important to understand that private property is also under a "social mortgage," meaning that property is to be used for the common good of all, because God created material goods for everyone.

(CSDC 176–184, 328–329)

220. What does the Bible say about money?

Money is a means of exchange, a measure of value and a reserve for the future. Money then is only a means: it must not become an end in itself. Jesus explicitly said: "You cannot serve God and mammon" (Mt 6:24). Money must never become an idol. Those who chase after money become its slave. On the other hand, money can be put to the service of God.

(CSDC 328; EG 55)

221. Are companies allowed to make profit?

Yes. Profit is a basic indication of a company's success, but it is not yet sufficient evidence that the company is truly serving the society.

To achieve sustainable development, the legitimate pursuit of profit must be in line with the fundamental protection of the dignity of the person. Profit achieved by means of exploitation or the violation of social justice and workers' rights is unjust.

(CSDC 340)

222. Is the "free market" a good thing?

Yes. In a free market, people freely offer and purchase goods and services within a legal and ethical framework. In a market economy, the consumers determine what is produced, at what price, and in what amount. The ethical market has proven itself to be capable of maintaining sustainable economic development in the long run. The Church values the advantages that the free market offers in making better use of resources. There are, however, other so-called "markets" that do not deserve to be called by this term because they are immoral, such as drug trafficking, human trafficking, the illegal arms trade, etc.

(CSDC 347)

223. The free market does not work without competition. But doesn't competition go against Christian charity?

It depends. Competition is the sporting desire to overcome one's rival, and an efficient means of achieving important objectives of justice: the lowering of prices, improving the response of entrepreneurs to the needs of consumers, and the more responsible use of resources. Competition rewards corporate effort, innovation, skills, etc. In this sense, competition is good. However, it is bad if it is conducted by unfair or unjust means (e.g., fraud), if the rules are rigged to unjustly favor one of the competitors, or when it is inspired by hatred.

(CSDC 347; CV 66)

224. So the free market has no limits and no other aim than making money?

No. The market is subject to ethical, legal, and cultural conditions and limits. For example, there are many priceless goods that are not marketable: human persons, their organs, and also friendship, forgiveness, family relationships, etc. The human person and his needs are the aim of the market. Unfortunately many people do not have access to the market and are unable to meet their most basic needs. In these cases, one must remember that the value and worth of a man is not dependent upon "*having something*," but comes simply from the fact that he or she "*is someone*": a human being, our brother or sister with inherent dignity. "It is a strict duty of justice and truth not to allow fundamental human needs to remain unsatisfied, and not to allow those burdened by such needs to perish" (CA 34).

(CSDC 348–350; CA 34)

225. Does government also play a role in the economy?

Yes. The government plays an important role in the economy. Its actions must be balanced, neither too intrusive nor too cautious, and must respect the principle of subsidiarity. This means that the main task of the government or the State in the economy is to create favorable conditions for the free exercise of economic activity, mainly by creating the legal framework for that activity, and by enabling self-help. Government should foster cooperation in "small units," such as the family, firms, and local communities, without replacing them, but rather allowing them to fulfill their duties by their own efforts as much as possible. When such self-help is not possible, the State should act according to the principle of solidarity and protect the most vulnerable.

(CSDC 336–337, 351–355; LS 129)

226. Are there other institutions that operate in the market, in addition to the public and private sectors?

There is an ever-greater number of institutions working in civil society based on economic principles which are formed and managed by private groups pursuing objectives of common interest. Many examples can be found in the provision of health care, assistance to the sick and elderly, neighborhood groups, groups promoting environmental conservation and protection, etc. These activities develop solidarity and are particularly important for the social fabric.

(CSDC 357; CV 39–40)

227. What is a business?

A business or firm is a unit of production that includes people, equipment, locations, money, etc.; but, above all, a firm is a "society of persons" (CA 43). A business must serve people by producing goods or providing services that are truly good and useful.

(CSDC 338; CA 43)

228. What is the relationship between companies, entrepreneurship, and virtue?

"When managed well, businesses actively enhance the dignity of employees and the development of virtues, such as solidarity, practical wisdom, justice, discipline, and many others. While the family is the first school of society, businesses, like many other social institutions, continue to educate people in virtue" (VBL 3).

(VBL 3)

229. Is success a priority in business?

Of course. In the first place, success consists in the efficient generation of profit, but it is not limited to this. A business is truly successful only if it creates a real sustainable value for people and for society, that is, the physical, mental, psychological, moral, and spiritual well-being of others. It is not enough for a business to redistribute part of its profits after wealth has been created, but it is first of all necessary that it produce human, social, and environmental value as a direct result of its economic activity and wealth creation. Success in the full sense of the word "is inextricably linked to this wider notion of well-being" (VBL 51).

(CSDC 332, 339–340)

230. Is trust important in business?

Yes. Trust is crucial for the functioning of the economy. Without it we would not dare sign a contract, buy a product, or join a company. Trust is gained through reliability and virtuous behavior, and is destroyed by sin.

(CSDC 343)

231. What virtues are particularly important in the economy?

The virtues are positive traits of character that help us to recognize the good and to accomplish it with inner freedom and joy. The most important human virtues are prudence, justice, fortitude, and temperance. Additionally, together with His sanctifying grace, God gives us the three theological virtues of faith, hope, and love. We need all of these for the economy, but in a particular way, the virtues of justice and charity are important in this field.

(CSDC 327, 343; YC 299–309)

232. How do we act with justice in the economy?

We act with justice by giving the other what is rightfully his. In the economy, this consists primarily in the faithful fulfillment of contracts, respecting agreements, the punctual delivery of goods in good condition, and making payments within the stipulated time. In order to be just, contracts must be free, that is, be entered into without deceit, fear, or coercion. Great economic inequality can lead to injustice if the negotiating partner with more power imposes conditions on the other.

(CCC 2411)

233. When is a price fair or just?

In principle, a price is fair or just when it is the outcome of free negotiations in the interplay between supply and demand. However, many factors can distort this free agreement: fraud, lack of information, monopolies of sellers or buyers, the extreme need of one of the partners, etc. All such forms of exploitation, along with disproportionate interest rates (usury), are sins against justice.

(CSDC 341, CCC 2414)

234. Love defines family and friendship. Does love also come into play in the economy?

Yes. The values of truth, justice, and freedom are born and grow from love. Without love, justice becomes hard and bitter. The economy is not a heartless machine that functions according to mechanical laws, but a meeting and exchange between people who are responsible for one another.

(CSDC 204–208)

235. Are there examples of this?

There are many. Numerous employers and employees go above and beyond what is required of them. They do so out of a sense of responsibility and love for their work and for the people that depend on their services. Investments can also be an act of generosity because investing means sacrificing immediate consumption and using funds to create jobs. Non-profit businesses that pursue social goals with an entrepreneurial spirit can be another manifestation of generosity, justice, and charity.

(CSDC 356–357)

236. In the economic world, what sins must be avoided?

All sins should be avoided, always and everywhere, in all areas of life, whether in business, politics, or one's private life. This is not an impossible or unrealistic standard, but a prerequisite for a happy life in society. In the economic life, one must be especially aware of greed, corruption, and all forms of injustice such as theft, fraud, usury, exploitation, etc.

(CCC 2408–2414)

237. Are the financial markets, banks, and speculative ventures structures of sin?

No. If they are oriented toward the common good, financial markets and banks provide an important service: they provide the money required by businesses and the economy (financial capital). For this reason, the debtor must pay interest as the price for availability of liquidity. Speculation can also be good, to the extent that it creates a balance between quantity and price among regions and between periods of shortage and abundance. Unfortunately, these financial instruments are often used incorrectly and irresponsibly, and therefore lose contact with the real economy. Financial markets become inflated because of irresponsible monetary and credit expansion.

(CSDC 368)

238. How can the situation be improved?

There is a need for conversion of hearts and the observance of ethical principles. The present situation also calls for full transparency of operations and for legal regulations of international financial markets within a uniform, binding legal framework.

(CSDC 369–372)

Special Topic: *Aging*

Elizabeth Reichert

239. Why is aging an important topic in today's world?

While large parts of the world continue to see steady population growth, many countries, especially in the Western world, are experiencing a dramatic shift in population demographics. As birthrates decline and life expectancies increase, populations are rapidly aging; this means that the percentage of working-age people drops as the percentage of retired people rises. As Pope John Paul II remarked, "the aging of the world's population is sure to be one of the most important features of the twenty-first century" (John Paul II, *Letter to the President of the Second World Assembly on Ageing* 2002).

240. What are some of the issues related to aging?

On a cultural and human level, the elderly face not only the sickness and suffering that come with age, but also isolation and neglect. As Pope Francis has stated, "the most serious privation that elderly persons undergo is not the weakening of the body and the disability that may ensue, but abandonment and exclusion, the privation of love." (Francis, *Message to the General Assembly of the Pontifical Academy for Life* 2014). On the economic level, aging gives rise to shortfalls in pension systems and increased health care costs.

241. How should this problem be addressed?

First, the "problem" is not the number of old people: "The elderly should never be considered a burden on society, but a resource which can contribute to society's well-being" (John Paul II, *Letter to the President of the Second World Assembly on Ageing* 2002). It is not simply a matter of what we can do *for* them, but what we can do together *with* them. In order to build a culture that promotes the dignity of every human person, "it will become more and more important to promote a widespread attitude of acceptance and appreciation of the elderly, and not relegate them to the fringes" (LEld 13).

(CSDC 222)

242. How should we treat the elderly?

We should honor them, as God Himself commands: "Honor your father and your mother, as the LORD, your God, has commanded you, that you may have a long life and that you may prosper in the land the LORD your God is giving you" (Dt 5:16). "Honoring older people involves a threefold duty: welcoming them, helping them and making good use of their qualities" (LEld 12).

243. Is the way we treat the elderly, the sick, and handicapped persons a measure of the humanity of a society?

Yes. "A society truly welcomes life when it recognizes that it is also precious in old age, in disability, in serious illness and even when it is fading; when it teaches that the call to human fulfillment does not exclude suffering; indeed, when it teaches its members to see in the sick and suffering a gift for the entire community, a presence that summons them to solidarity and responsibility. This is the Gospel of life..." (Francis, *Message to the General Assembly of the Pontifical Academy for Life* 2014).

244. Does the Church offer any solutions to the problems surrounding pension systems?

While it is not the role of the Church to propose specific suggestions, she does delineate important relevant principles. First of all, "in responding to this question, we must not be guided chiefly by economic criteria; rather, we must be inspired by sound moral principles" (John Paul II, *Letter to the President of the Second World Assembly on Ageing* 2002). More concretely, this issue demands the proper application of *both* the principles of solidarity *and* subsidiarity. On the one hand, the principle of solidarity moves us to recognize the dignity of each person rather than basing his or her worth on mere utility. It calls us to look out for our brothers and sisters, seeing that they receive the care they need. On the other hand, solidarity without subsidiarity leads to a "welfare state." State intervention, when it is required by the common good, should be limited, and support families and communities at a lower order because "needs are best understood and satisfied by people who are closest to them" (CA 48).

(CSDC 187–188, CA 48)

8 Political Life: *Peace, Freedom, and Justice in Society*

MARTIN SCHLAG

A good Christian participates actively in political life and prays for the politicians that they may love their people and serve them with humility.
SEE POPE FRANCIS, *MORNING MEDITATION*,
SEPTEMBER 16, 2013

Modern nations are very complex. Politics and politicians have the high calling to serve the common good of their countries. Their service is a way of putting charity into practice. The Church does not identify herself with a single political party nor does she propose a specific path; rather, she proclaims those principles and values that order political life toward its foundation and purpose: the human person.

245. What is politics good for?

Everyone lives in communities: families, associations, neighborhoods, and so on. At the highest level of social organization we live in nations. Politics serves to unite and order a multitude of people with different needs and interests, seeking their common good.

246. What is a nation?

A nation consists of a group of people living together in a common territory and governed by a political authority. Nations are also called States.

247. What forms of nations or States are there?

There are monarchies, in which political authority is exercised by only one person, the monarch. There are aristocracies, in which the authority is shared among a small ruling group. And there are democracies, in which the political authority resides in the population at large. They exercise their authority either indirectly through representatives or directly by the vote.

248. What does Jesus teach about politics?

"Jesus said to them, 'Repay to Caesar what belongs to Caesar and to God what belongs to God'" (Mk 12:17; cf. Mt 22:15–22, Lk 20:20–26). In affirming this, Jesus implicitly condemned "every attempt at making temporal power divine or absolute: God alone can demand everything from man. At the same time, temporal power has the right to its due: Jesus does not consider it unjust to pay taxes to Caesar" (CSDC 379).

(CSDC 379)

249. What do St. Paul and other biblical witnesses write about politics?

We should obey legitimate authority "because of conscience" (Rom 13:5) as an order established by God. The Apostle certainly does not intend to legitimize every existing authority, but rather teaches that political power ought to guarantee "that we may lead a quiet and tranquil life in all devotion and dignity" (1 Tim 2:2).

(CSDC 380–381)

250. Summing up, what does the Bible as a whole teach about political authority?

"The biblical message provides endless inspiration for Christian reflection on political power, recalling that it comes from God and is an integral part of the order that he created. This order is perceived by the human conscience and, in social life, finds its fulfillment in the truth, justice, freedom and solidarity that bring peace"[1] (CSDC 383).

(CSDC 383)

251. What is the basis and purpose of political authority?

The foundation and purpose of all political life and activity is the human person. The political community is based on the moral law that God has imprinted on our human nature. Our conscience reveals this moral order to us, and obedience to it is the key to achieving the common good.

(CSDC 384)

252. Can't I become happy on my own? Do I have to live in a political community?

Each one of us is free to pursue his or her own happiness. However, living in a nation—which implies living in a political community—is natural for us. It helps us achieve our full growth as human persons. By cooperating in the attainment of the common good we flourish: the human person is not only an autonomous individual bent on his or her own interests but becomes him or herself in relationship to others.

(CSDC 384)

253. How can we define the people of a nation?

The most important characteristics of a people are a shared life and shared values, which are the source of communion on the spiritual and moral level.

(CSDC 386)

254. What should a nation grant its people?

The aim of political life is the attainment of the common good, consisting of peace, freedom, and justice for all. The political authority of a nation must recognize and respect human dignity by defending and promoting fundamental and inalienable human rights, which must not be sacrificed for the common good. It is also necessary that each individual citizen fulfills his or her own corresponding duties.

(CSDC 388–389)

255. What are human rights?

Human rights grant protection against the power of the government. Certain spheres of life must not be infringed by governmental authority: life, liberty, property, religious beliefs, conscience, etc. In the course of time, many such rights have been upheld. Since the Second World War, a new kind of human rights relating to social protection and security has evolved. Such "rights" should rather be called "programmatic norms" or political goals; this is because they cannot be demanded by way of law (for example, one cannot demand that the government provide a job), but rather they serve as goals for policies that will foster their attainment. They include the right to work, to education, to health care, and so forth.

256. What is the origin of human rights and what characterizes them?

Human rights are rooted in the dignity of each and every human being. These rights are universal, inviolable, and inalienable. As they are not granted by the mere will of men, by public powers, or by the State, nobody can be deprived of his or her human rights. To the contrary, individuals must respect other persons' human rights, and public authority must guarantee them.

(CSDC 153)

257. Does the Church proclaim human rights?

"By virtue of the Gospel committed to her, [the Church] proclaims the rights of man" (GS 41). By acknowledging human rights, the Church sees an extraordinary opportunity to recognize human dignity more effectively and to promote it universally as a characteristic inscribed by God the Creator on every man and every woman.

(CSDC 152)

258. Wouldn't it be rather selfish to demand rights only for oneself?

Yes. Actually, the Church underlines the connection between

rights and duties. It would be a contradiction to claim rights for oneself that one denies to others. Every right also entails a corresponding responsibility. "Those, therefore, who claim their own rights, yet altogether forget or neglect to carry out their respective duties, are people who build with one hand and destroy with the other" (CSDC 156, quoting PT 30). An excessive affirmation of rights can give rise to an exaggerated individualism that ignores the common good.

(CSDC 156, 158)

259. Do minorities have special rights within a nation?

The Church affirms that minorities possess precise rights and duties, and above all, the right to exist. Moreover, minorities have the right to maintain their cultures, including their languages, and to maintain their religious beliefs, including worship services.

(CSDC 387)

260. What does the Church teach about democracy?

"The Church values the democratic system inasmuch as it ensures the participation of citizens in making political choices, guarantees to the governed the possibility both of electing and holding accountable those who govern them, and of replacing them through peaceful means when appropriate" (CA 46).

(CSDC 406; CA 46)

261. In a democracy, the majority makes the laws. Can the majority, morally speaking, pass whatever laws it desires?

No, a democracy must not destroy the foundational values on which it is built. These are: "the dignity of every human person, the respect of human rights, [and] commitment to the common good as the purpose and guiding criterion for political life. If there is no general consensus on these values, the deepest meaning of democracy is lost and its stability is compromised" (CSDC 407).

(CSDC 397–398, 407)

262. What is "ethical relativism"?

Ethical relativism is the belief that there are no objective or universal criteria for establishing moral norms. According to the Church's social doctrine, ethical relativism is one of the greatest threats to modern-day democracies.

(CSDC 407)

263. In addition to the important values of human dignity and human rights, is there anything else that democracy needs to exist?

Yes. Democracy needs institutions. These institutions include free and general elections, the separation of powers, accountability of politicians to the people, independent and impartial judges, and lawful public administration. The Church acknowledges their importance.

(CSDC 408)

264. Are political parties important for democracy?

Yes. Political parties are beneficial for democracy. They "have the task of fostering widespread participation and making public responsibilities accessible to all" (CSDC 413). They must always pursue the common good of the whole nation, and not only the interests of their electorate.

(CSDC 413)

265. What is "civil society"?

Civil society refers to those relationships and resources that are relatively independent from the political sphere and have not been absorbed by the State. It consists of the network of human relationships, associations, corporations, and institutions that have a social purpose but are not run by the government. The principle of subsidiarity protects the integrity of civil society. Solidarity too finds its natural home in civil society, as it builds up the whole of society, including the political sphere.

(CSDC 417–420; CV 39)

266. Is there a difference between political power and political authority?

Yes. Power is force that can be used for both good and evil. Political authority is power directed exclusively toward the common good.

267. When is political authority exercised in a legitimate way?

"Authority is exercised legitimately when it acts for the common good and employs morally licit means to attain it" (CompCCC 406). Political authority must guarantee an ordered community life without usurping the free activity of individuals and groups. When orienting this freedom toward the common good, it must respect and defend the independence of individual and social subjects.

(CSDC 394)

268. Are just laws and commands morally binding?

Yes. When the political authority issues just laws, orders, and commands, we are obliged in conscience to obey them. If not, one "opposes what God has appointed" (Rom 13:2) and commits a sin.

(CSDC 398)

269. Why can political authority create morally binding laws? Where does this moral force of the legislative power come from?

All of the moral force of the political authority comes from its being exercised for good purposes and by use of means that are not only efficient but also morally acceptable. The political authority "should respect the principle of the 'rule of law' in which the law, and not the arbitrary will of some, is sovereign. Unjust laws and measures contrary to the moral order are not binding in conscience" (CompCCC 406). In such a case they cease to be law and instead become acts of violence.

(CSDC 396, 398)

270. How should citizens react to immoral civil laws?

"Citizens are not obligated in conscience to follow the prescriptions of civil authorities if their precepts are contrary to the demands of the moral order, to the fundamental rights of persons or to the teachings of the Gospel"[2] (CSDC 399). When morally upright people are called to cooperate in morally evil acts, they must refuse. It is a grave duty of conscience not to cooperate in practices that, although permitted by civil legislation, are contrary to the law of God.

(CSDC 399)

271. Do citizens have a right to resist political authority?

"It is legitimate to resist authority should it violate in a serious or repeated manner the essential principles of natural law" (CSDC 400). Even though the church recommends passive resistance, armed resistance can be legitimate against manifest tyranny, which does great damage to fundamental personal rights and to the common good of the country.

(CSDC 400–401)

272. What is the role of the judicial power?

The role of the judicial power, exercised by independent judges in the courts, is to administer justice to citizens according to the law. Judges must seek truth impartially, and give each party its due according to the law. Cases should be dealt with as swiftly as possible. Legal disputes between opposing parties are inevitable in any society, but in fulfilling their task well, judges bring peace and harmony to the people of a nation.

(CSDC 402)

273. Are judges also required to punish crimes?

Yes. In the courts of criminal law, judges must punish criminals who have been convicted in a fair and just trial according to the law. Punishment is only just if it is based on written law enacted prior to the committed deed. Moreover, it must be reasonably proven that the person is in fact guilty of the crime.

274. What is the purpose of criminal punishment?

The punishment of criminals serves the purpose of restoring the order of justice, defending the public order, and guaranteeing the safety of persons. It is furthermore an instrument for the correction of the offender. The way the criminal punishment is carried out should facilitate the re-introduction of the convicted person into society.

(CSDC 403)

275. How are the accused and prisoners to be treated?

Accused offenders and prisoners must be treated in conformity with their human dignity. They must not be subjected to degrading treatment. No person can be imprisoned without a trial, and the trial must not be delayed. "Officials of the court are especially called to exercise due discretion in their investigations so as not to violate the rights of the accused to confidentiality and in order not to undermine the principle of the presumption of innocence" (CSDC 404).

(CSDC 404)

276. May torture be used in extreme cases?

No. Torture must never be used. Neither circumstances nor motives can justify torture.

(CSDC 404)

277. Is the death penalty a legitimate form of criminal punishment?

Modern society has the means to suppress crime without turning to the death penalty, by imprisoning and thus incapacitating criminals without denying them the chance to reform. "The Church sees as a sign of hope 'a growing public opposition to the death penalty, even when such a penalty is seen as a kind of "legitimate defense" on the part of society'"[3] (CSDC 405).

(CSDC 405; EV 27; CCC 2266–2267; AL 83)

278. What is the purpose of the executive power, especially of public administration?

The public administration at any level is oriented toward the service of citizens and is guided by the law. The State should act as a steward of the common good.

(CSDC 412)

279. Do civil servants need special virtues?

Yes. Responsible authority requires those virtues that make it possible to exercise power in the service of the people (patience, modesty, moderation, charity, and so on). Such authority is "exercised by persons who are able to accept the common good, and not prestige or the gaining of personal advantages, as the true goal of their work" (CSDC 410).

(CSDC 410)

280. Should Catholics engage in politics?

Every Christian is called to attend to temporal affairs, and to practice justice and charity at the service of the common good of society in a manner corresponding to his or her vocation. For example, responsibility for the common good makes it morally obligatory to exercise the right to vote. At the same time, "not everyone is called to engage directly in political life. Society is also enriched by a countless array of organizations which work to promote the common good and to defend the environment, whether natural or urban" (LS 232).

(CCC 1913–1915, 2240; LS 232)

281. Can working in politics be a vocation?

Men and women who possess the personal qualities for political life and feel inclined to political activity can be certain that they have received a high calling from God. Politics can be a path of justice and charity.

(CV 7)

282. Are Catholics free to follow their conscience in politics, or are they bound to a specific "political program"?

Catholics are free to follow their conscience in politics. No political program is imposed by the Magisterium of the Church; not even her social teachings constitute such a program because the church does not offer technical solutions. Catholics display a healthy pluralism when they take different positions on a number of political issues. However, certain values based on natural law are common to all people of good will, and therefore also to Catholics. These values, which are not negotiable, include: the right to life from conception to natural death; the nature of marriage as an indissoluble bond between one man and one woman; the right of parents to secure the education they deem fit for their children; the need to promote social justice; the development of an economy at the service of the common good, and similar considerations.

(CDF, *Doctrinal Note on Some Questions Regarding the Participation of Catholics in Political Life* 2002)

283. How does the Catholic Church relate to the State?

The relationship of the Catholic Church with the State can be summarized as simultaneously independent and cooperative. Both the Church and the political community manifest themselves in visible organizational structures that pursue different ends: the State serves the temporal common good, the Church the spiritual good. Even though the institutions are thus separate, they should cooperate in the service of the human person, who has both temporal and spiritual dimensions. Furthermore, the Church also contributes to the attainment of the temporal common good when she pursues her salvific mission.

(CSDC 424–425)

284. Does the Church teach religious freedom?

Yes. The Catholic Church promotes "the right of the person and of communities to social and civil freedom in matters religious," as indicated in the title of *Dignitatis Humanae*. Such a right must be recognized and sanctioned as a civil right to be exercised within the limits of the public order. "Society and the State must not force a person to act against his conscience or prevent him from acting in conformity with it.[4] Religious freedom is not a moral license to adhere to error, nor as an implicit right to error"[5] (CSDC 421).

(CSDC 421–423)

285. What are the main threats to religious freedom today?

The main threats to religious freedom today stem from religious extremism, especially from violent Islamic fundamentalists, and from the subtle but nevertheless violent attempt to exclude religion from the public sphere in Western countries. This amounts to the imposition of atheism as a new form of civil religion. (cf. Benedict XVI, *Message for the World Day of Peace* 2011)

9 The Family of Nations

MARTIN SCHLAG

Human interdependence is increasing and gradually spreading throughout the world. The unity of the human family, embracing people who enjoy equal natural dignity, implies a universal common good. This good calls for an organization of the community of nations able to "provide for the different needs of men."
CATECHISM OF THE CATHOLIC CHURCH, 1911,
QUOTING GS 84 §2

We live in a globalized world. No nation can live isolated from the rest. Political decisions taken in one country often affect its neighbors. In this family of nations, international law and coordinated measures help us to progress forward on the path of peace and development.

286. Since we all live in our own nations with their own needs and difficulties, why should we be concerned about other nations?

We need to care about other nations because all men and women on earth form the one family of God, and as brothers and sisters we share a common destiny and are responsible for one another. We belong to various races and speak different languages, but we are all children of God. Thus the various nations together form one international community.

287. What does the Bible say about the family of nations?

What the Bible tells us about creation manifests the unity of the human family and teaches us that God is our loving Father and the

Lord of history. It also reveals that sin is the cause of division among peoples. Furthermore, it is part of the plan of salvation and part of the mission of the Church that this fragmented, scattered reality be brought back together through the Holy Spirit. For those who live a new life in Christ, racial and cultural differences must no longer be causes of division.

(CSDC 429–431)

288. What does the Christian message mean for the international community?

The international community must strive, over and over again, to achieve the unity willed by the Creator. Reaching this communion of nations cannot be a result of violence but rather of a moral and cultural effort.

(CSDC 432)

289. How can this unity among nations come about?

Unity can only be achieved if the dignity of every person, in all of the person's various dimensions (material and spiritual, individual and communal), is universally recognized; if the human relationships in and between the various nations are based on the guiding values of freedom and truth, justice and charity; and if, by general agreement, the international community seeks to promote the universal common good. We all share the same planet, its climate and air, its oceans, and routes of transport. We are increasingly connected, and we can thus only live together in peace, liberty, and justice if we make a common effort to jointly construct institutions that protect these values. This is what we call the universal common good.

(CSDC 433)

290. What does the "sovereignty" of a nation mean?

Sovereignty means that every nation is an independent and free subject of international law. The relationship among sovereign nations is characterized by equality, mutual trust, support, and respect.

Sovereignty, therefore, is not absolute. It must not be used to justify attempts to subordinate other nations.

(CSDC 434–435)

291. How is the relationship among sovereign nations regulated?

The relationship among free and sovereign nations is regulated by the law of nations and by principles of the universal moral law that are written on the human heart as a living expression of the shared conscience of humanity.

(CSDC 436)

292. Why is the law of nations or international law necessary?

To resolve the tensions that arise among different political communities, which can compromise the stability of nations and international security, it is indispensable to make use of common rules together with a commitment to negotiation, and to definitively reject the idea that international disputes can be solved through recourse to war. International law is the result of the quest for peace and stability among nations.

(CSDC 438)

293. Why isn't international law sufficient in itself?

International law is not enough to ensure lasting peace because the principle of mutual confidence is of the utmost importance in consolidating law, and confidence is based on shared moral values. "Universal respect of the principles underlying 'a legal structure in conformity with the moral order'[1] is a necessary condition for the stability of international life" (CSDC 437).

(CSDC 433, 437, 439)

294. What does the Church say about the existing international organizations?

In general, the Church views the role of intergovernmental organizations positively. "Because of the globalization of problems, it has become more urgent than ever to stimulate international political action that pursues the goals of peace and development through the adoption of coordinated measures"[2] (CSDC 442). This does not mean that the Church endorses policies that address problems in a way that is contrary to the gospel and the dignity of the human person.

(CSDC 440–442)

295. Is the Holy See also a member of the international community?

Yes. The Holy See is a subject of international law. This means it is "a sovereign authority that performs acts which are juridically its own. It exercises an external sovereignty recognized within the context of the international community" (CSDC 444) in order to carry out its mission.

(CSDC 444)

296. Are richer nations required to help poorer nations develop?

Yes. "The Church's social doctrine encourages forms of cooperation that are capable of facilitating access to the international market on the part of countries suffering from poverty and underdevelopment" (CSDC 447). "The spirit of international cooperation requires that, beyond the strict market mentality, there should be an awareness of the duty to solidarity, justice and universal charity"[3] (CSDC 448).

(CSDC 446–448)

297. Does the Church offer a certain model or concrete plan of action for international development?

No, the Church leaves the technical solutions and concrete plans of action to the men and women of good will who actively shape public life. However, she lifts her prophetic voice, proclaiming that "the need to resolve the structural causes of poverty cannot be delayed, not only for the pragmatic reason of its urgency for the good order of society, but because society needs to be cured of a sickness which is weakening and frustrating it, and which can only lead to new crises. Welfare projects, which meet certain urgent needs, should be considered merely temporary responses" (EG 202).

(EG 202)

10 Safeguarding the Environment

MARTIN SCHLAG AND ELIZABETH REICHERT

Triune Lord, wondrous community of infinite love,
teach us to contemplate you
in the beauty of the universe,
for all things speak of you.
Awaken our praise and thankfulness
for every being that you have made.
Give us the grace to feel profoundly joined
to everything that is.

POPE FRANCIS, *LAUDATO SI'*
(A PRAYER FOR OUR EARTH), 246

"We are all responsible for the protection and care of the environment. This responsibility knows no boundaries" (Benedict XVI, *Message for the World Day of Peace* 2010, 11). All of creation is a gift of God and every creature is a unique manifestation of God's glory. We are thus called to approach creation with an attitude of gratitude and appreciation, avoiding both the extremes of the idolatry of nature and the idolatry of human power. The Church thus proposes an "integral ecology," which values and respects both its human and natural elements.

298. What does the Bible teach about the created world and man's place in it?

Creation is an object of constant praise in the Old Testament. The world is not a hostile environment, but a gift of God where God Himself is present. The world, in fact, reveals the mystery of God who created and sustains it in harmony. "God has written a precious book, 'whose letters are the multitude of created things present in the universe'"[1] (LS 85); and we will correctly understand this book only if we know its author. As the creation account tells us, God made all things and "saw that it was good" (Gen 1:25). At the summit of this creation, God placed man and woman, the only creatures made "in his image" (Gen 1:27), and He entrusted all of creation to their responsibility.

(CSDC 451–452, 456; LS 65–92)

299. Does this mean that man can use nature as he desires?

"The attitude that must characterize the way man acts in relation to creation is essentially one of gratitude and appreciation....If the relationship with God is placed aside, nature is stripped of its profound meaning and impoverished" (CSDC 487). Man must not set himself in the place of God, but remember that he is a "cooperator" with God in the work of creation; thus, only in dialogue with God do we find the truth from which we can draw inspiration and norms to foster the development of creation as God intended.

(CSDC 452, 460, 487)

300. What was Jesus' relationship to nature?

Christ as God's Divine Word is the Creator of all things. He then became man Himself and with human eyes beheld the beauty of creation. He made use of natural elements. He spoke of nature in images and parables, but He also dominated it (for instance when He calmed the storm, cf. Mt 14:22–33). "The Lord puts nature at the service of his plan of redemption. He asks his disciples to look at things, at the seasons and at people with the trust of children who know that they will never be abandoned by a provident Father (cf. Lk 11:11–13)" (CSDC 453). And in a special way, in the sacraments, "nature is taken up by God to become a means of mediating supernatural life" (LS 235).

(CSDC 453; LS 96–100, 235)

301. Does Christ's redemption extend to nature too?

The world was wounded by sin, but Jesus inaugurates a new world and "creates anew those relationships of order and harmony that sin had destroyed" (CSDC 454). The whole of creation takes part in the renewal brought about by the death and resurrection of the Lord, even though it has not yet become fully manifest. The children of God participate in the redemption of nature through their sanctified work. After His resurrection, the gaze of Jesus is constantly on creation, and we can behold Him through the reflection of His beauty in nature.

(CSDC 453–455; LS 99–100)

302. How does the Christian faith explain the abuses of nature committed by mankind?

The Bible shows us that the ultimate reason for all abuses of nature is sin. As a consequence of sin, nature turns against man, and man against nature. Many have come to consider nature as a resource that may be conquered and exploited at will and without ethical considerations, without responsibility for future generations, or respect for nature as a home to all of mankind. We at times behave as if there were unlimited reserves of energy at our disposal, and do not consider the negative effects of pollution. Nature then appears as an instrument in the hands of man that he can manipulate, especially by means of technology. This is a reductionist conception of the natural world. It views nature in mechanistic and consumeristic terms. This is "ecological sin," which calls for an "ecological conversion."

(CSDC 453, 461–462; LS 8, 217)

303. Does this mean the Church blames science and technology for the abuse of nature?

No, the results of science and technology are in themselves positive because men and women have extended their mastery over nearly the whole of nature and continue to do so. Christians are convinced that the triumphs of the human race are a sign of God's grace. As long as scientific progress is used for the true good of humanity, the Church is in no way opposed to such progress; rather, she considers science and technology to be "a wonderful product of a God-given human creativity, since they have provided us with wonderful possibilities, and we all gratefully benefit from them"[2] (CSDC 457).

(CSDC 456–457; LS 102–103, 131)

304. Under what circumstances does progress become part of humanity's true good?

Not every increase in human power over nature is progress. We do not know in detail what God's plan for the future of mankind is, or where developments are heading. However, God has given us moral laws to guide our actions, our research, and the technology through which we dominate nature. Abiding by them always leads to humanity's true good. Generally speaking, these laws consist in the respect for human dignity and for the rest of creation. Respect for human dignity implies that human beings must never be used as mere means. Respect for nature entails that we intervene so as to foster its development in its own way of being, as God created it, not to destroy it.

(CSDC 458–460; LS 105)

305. What are some of the man-made problems the Church has addressed?

The Church is especially concerned about air, soil, and water pollution, and about waste and the throwaway culture predominant in many of our societies. The Church has addressed climate change, the carbon cycle, and the loss of biodiversity. These problems in nature lead to a decline in the quality of human life and to the breakdown of society, and they are made worse by global inequality and the sometimes ineffectual responses of the international community.

(LS 20–59)

306. Why does the Church see the loss of biodiversity as a problem?

The extinction of species affects the surrounding ecosystem and means the loss of important resources for food, medicine, and other things. "It is not enough, however, to think of different species merely as potential 'resources' to be exploited, while overlooking the fact that they have value in themselves" (LS 33). Each species manifests God's glory in its own unique way and we have no right to carelessly eradicate them.

(LS 32–42, 84–87)

307. What does the Church say about the climate and climate change?

The Church appeals to scientists, consumers, and those engaged in industrial activity to develop a greater sense of responsibility for the effects of their behavior on the climate. "The climate is a common good, belonging to all and meant for all. At the global level, it is a complex system linked to many of the essential conditions for human life. A very solid scientific consensus indicates that we are presently witnessing a disturbing warming of the climatic system" (LS 23).

(CSDC 470; LS 23–26)

308. Does the Church offer specific technical solutions for the environmental crisis?

"On many concrete questions, the Church has no reason to offer a definitive opinion; she knows that honest debate must be encouraged among experts, while respecting divergent views" (LS 61). However, the Church urges against the extreme positions of the idolatry of human power which denies any need for environmental commitment on the one hand, and of the idolatry of nature which proposes the idea that all human interventions are a threat on the other.

(LS 60–61)

309. What does the idolatry of human power mean?

The idolatry of human power means reducing nature in a utilitarian way to a mere object that can be manipulated and exploited. This is not the result of science and technological research, but of "scientism" and technocratic ideologies that accept no limits. Not everything that can be done technically may be done ethically. Moral limits and conditions exist: God's law, and the respect for the transcendent dimension of the human person and of creation itself must guide our actions.

(CSDC 462; LS 106–114)

310. What does the idolatry of nature mean?

It means going so far as to divinize nature or the earth. It makes an idol of creation and creates imbalances where, for example, "more zeal is shown in protecting other species than in defending the dignity which all human beings share in equal measure" (LS 90). The Church opposes ecocentrism and biocentrism because she believes in man's superior dignity over and responsibility for all other living beings. That is why concern for ecology should always be connected with a concern for "human ecology," that is, with the protection of human life and families.

(CSDC 463–464; LS 90–92)

311. Is there a middle path?

There are several possible paths between these extremes that should enter into dialogue with each other in order to find a solution. "Discussions are needed in which all those directly or indirectly affected...can make known their problems and concerns, and have access to adequate and reliable information in order to make decisions for the common good, present and future" (LS 135).

We must learn not to think in exclusive dichotomies; rather, we must seek inclusive alternatives. Very frequently the decision is not "either/or" but "both/and." In this respect, the Church proposes the idea of an "integral ecology."

(LS 135)

312. What is an "integral ecology"?

An integral ecology recognizes that we are a part of nature; and therefore "the human environment and the natural environment deteriorate together" (LS 50). Our attitude toward human beings affects our attitude toward creation and vice-versa. When we are deaf to the cry of the poor, it is difficult to hear the cry of nature. "There can be no renewal of our relationship with nature without a renewal of humanity itself" (LS 118). An integral ecology is one that respects both human and social dimensions; it recognizes that everything is connected. It consists of a broader vision that considers ecological, social, and economic concerns in making decisions.

(LS 48–49, 117–121, 138–142)

313. How does concern for the environment fit into the operation of our economic institutions?

As part of this integral ecology, Pope Francis has called for an "economic ecology" that would consider all the costs involved in its decisions, including "the economic and social costs of using up shared environmental resources" (CV 50). In the long run, environmental protection is also economically advantageous because an economy that destroys the environment in which it exists negatively affects the production of wealth. In the short and medium term it might seem more advantageous to generate profit at the expense of the environment (e.g., through pollution, depletion of natural resources, destruction of biodiversity). The consequences of these so-called "negative externalities" must be reduced, and in turn we must seek innovative ways to reduce the environmental impact of production and encourage the responsible consumption of goods.

(CSDC 470; CV 50; LS 138–142, 183–196)

314. Is there a link between poverty and ecological damage?

Yes. The environmental crisis affects those who are poorest in a particularly harsh and dramatic way. Erosion and desertification, rising sea levels, armed conflicts and forced emigration, and the lack of the economic and technological means to confront epidemics, pollution, and other calamities have their greatest effect on the poor. Many people live in the polluted suburbs of large cities, in makeshift residences or in huge complexes that are crumbling and unsafe. These facts create an urgent need for economic and ecological development.

(CSDC 482; LS 48–52, 150–153)

315. Taking into consideration the overpopulation in many of these urban areas, would it not be a solution to reduce the number of births?

No, demographic growth is fully compatible with integral economic development. Environmental concern must not become a pretext for political and economic decisions that would be at odds with the dignity of the human person. "How can we genuinely teach the importance of concern for other vulnerable beings, however troublesome or inconvenient they may be, if we fail to protect a human embryo, even when its presence is uncomfortable and creates difficulties?" (LS 120) Developmental aid by international organizations or States must not be conditioned on the introduction of sterilization or abortion programs or other immoral measures.

(CSDC 483; LS 50, 91, 120)

316. Ecological damage often affects indigenous people. Do they have a special right to protection or must they simply accede to progress?

Indigenous peoples have a special relationship to their lands because the very meaning of their existence is tied to them. This relationship therefore deserves particular attention, and must be appropriately protected.

(CSDC 471; LS 146)

317. What is environmental sustainability?

Environmental sustainability means using today's resources in a way that our present needs are satisfied while also seeing to it that future generations will be able to satisfy theirs. There are a number of scientific disciplines that study the different aspects of ecological sustainability and sustainable development. The Church encourages these studies because responsibility for the environment, which is the common heritage of mankind, extends not only to present needs but also to those of the future.

(CSDC 467; LS 159–161)

318. What does the Church say about biotechnology, especially genetically modified organisms?

"It is difficult to make a general judgment about genetic modification (GM), whether vegetable or animal, medical or agricultural, since these vary greatly among themselves and call for specific considerations" (LS 133). The Christian faith tells us that man may intervene in creation, including in the genetic code of living beings. At the same time, the Church strongly urges responsibility because nature is a gift entrusted by the Creator to the intelligence and moral responsibility of men and women. We may improve living beings or their natural environment but not damage them. It is necessary to accurately evaluate the real benefits as well as the possible risks on the organisms themselves, the social and economic consequences, and the long-term effects on human beings and the surrounding ecosystem. Acting lightly or irresponsibly in such matters is unacceptable.

(CSDC 458–460, 472–480; LS 132–136)

319. Do the principles of solidarity and subsidiarity pertain to the use of biotechnology in developing countries?

The spirit of international solidarity will promote the exchange of scientific and technological knowledge and the transfer of technologies to developing countries in order to help them develop their own scientific and technological institutions. At the same time, the principle of subsidiarity appeals to political leaders of the developing countries to do everything in their power to develop on their own, with their own means and strength. An important effort in this process of development is combatting corruption and promoting trade policies that are favorable to their people, giving special attention to the particular characteristics and needs of their countries.

(CSDC 474–476)

320. Does the State have a responsibility to intervene in the protection of the environment?

Yes. The State must enact legal rules to protect the environment. The earth's population possesses the right to a safe and healthy natural environment. This implies the legal duty of national and international authorities to protect the environment at a juridical level.

(CSDC 468–469)

321. Is State intervention necessary at the international level?

Yes. The Church hopes for a "change of direction," and calls on the international community to enter into an effective dialogue on the environment because "interdependence obliges us to think of *one world with a common plan*" (LS 164).

(LS 163–164)

322. And in domestic politics?

Politicians should not only think in the short term in order to win elections: "True statecraft is manifest when, in difficult times, we uphold high principles and think of the long-term common good" (LS 178). We sorely need healthy politics "capable of reforming and coordinating institutions, promoting best practices and overcoming undue pressure and bureaucratic inertia. It should be added, though, that even the best mechanisms can break down when there are no worthy goals and values, or a genuine and profound humanism to serve as the basis of a noble and generous society" (LS 181). When government licenses are required, "environmental impact assessment should....be part of the process from the beginning, and be carried out in a way which is interdisciplinary, transparent and free of all economic or political pressure" (LS 183).

(LS 178–183)

323. What is the appropriate reaction of a Christian to the frightening prospects of environmental destruction?

The serious ecological problems we face are "a summons to profound interior conversion" (LS 217). They call for new lifestyles inspired by sobriety, temperance, humility, and self-discipline at both the individual and social levels. These virtues liberate and give hope and joy. We must therefore break with the logic of mere consumption ("consumerism") and promote forms of agricultural and industrial production that respect the order of creation and satisfy the basic human needs of all. We should also create awareness, helping consumers to understand their social responsibility, and develop education in "ecological citizenship."

(CSDC 486; LS 206–211, 216–224)

Special Topic: *Hunger*

Tebaldo Vinciguerra

324. Is hunger still a problem?

Hunger is a grave problem. According to the Food and Agriculture Organization, about 795 million people were undernourished in the world in 2015. The majority of these people live in developing countries, primarily in Asia and Africa. Within these countries, it is often in rural areas that the population is most affected by hunger.

(L&F 6, 9)

325. What is the difference between hunger and malnutrition?

Hunger means an insufficient calorie intake. Malnutrition refers to an imbalanced diet; for example, lacking in vitamins and minerals (with serious repercussions on health and intellectual development) or consumption of excessive amounts of carbohydrates (which is a factor in diabetes and obesity). Malnutrition affects over two billion people in the world. Most of these people do not have access to a balanced and varied diet due to poverty, while others—though affluent—are uneducated on these issues. It is crucial to protect against malnutrition in the earliest years, as the negative effects can be lifelong.

(L&F 7–8)

326. What are the sources of food waste?

A considerable part of the food that is produced goes bad shortly after harvest as many areas are unable to preserve it or bring it to the market. In these cases we speak of "post-harvest losses" rather than waste. Examples of food waste include the massive volume of fish thrown out by fishing boats because only certain parts are used, waste in the various stages of processing and distribution, and uneaten food thrown out by consumers. There is often a considerable difference in the food waste in poor countries and rich countries (where people often throw out their own body weight in food each year).

(L&F 56)

327. What are some of the issues surrounding food production today?

More and more, we know "what" to do: we have developed irrigation systems and techniques of food preservation, and we understand the steps needed to develop small agricultural businesses and the dangers of certain farming practices. The situation, though, remains problematic, as may be seen in the number of people that lack food; the number of communities previously suffering from hunger that now suffer from malnutrition due to the spread of poor eating habits; poverty in the areas where food is produced; the generalized specialization and concentration of food production on a global level; and the slow processes of access to title deeds for land in rural and indigenous communities. These problems are not new. The impression is thus that the situation continues because of a "lack of will."

(L&F 13–14, 16–25)

328. What are the major approaches to food production?

Simplifying things, there are two contrasting approaches: on the one hand, there is production that is intensive and extensive, highly mechanized, and based on sophisticated research (chemical, genetic, biotechnological, and so on). On the other hand, there is production at the local or family level, which places value on biodiversity and natural local species ("agroecology" and "family agriculture" are emblematic terms of this approach). It is necessary to continue forward without a closed ideological mentality, continually evaluating various initiatives, and encouraging those initiatives that best contribute to human development, the environment, food quality, an inclusive economy, and a fair distribution of profits.

329. What can nations do about hunger and about food in general?

At the national level, each country must adopt appropriate policies to order the economy so that each person has the opportunity to work and consequently to obtain food, and to use its own natural resources in a sustainable way. Policies that support food producers are also needed, such as adequate training and access to markets, credit, and technology.

Concern for food and nutrition is also a duty of governments. This includes educating those who choose and prepare foods, and also holding responsible producers of food (to maintain high product quality and ensure decent working conditions at all levels of the supply chain) and those who work in advertising (so they do not promote food or eating habits that could be harmful to people's health). These policies will of course vary from country to country, depending on the level of development and the agricultural, political, climatic and cultural context.

(L&F 14, 116–118, 121–122, 129–140)

330. And at the international level?

Actions at the international level are essential for coordination. Pope Francis wrote, "The problem is that we still lack the culture needed to confront this crisis. We lack leadership capable of striking out on new paths and meeting the needs of the present with concern for all and without prejudice towards coming generations....It is remarkable how weak international political responses have been" (LS 53–54). International action is more necessary than ever in order to balance trade policies, particularly to enable the least developed countries to strengthen their agricultural sectors, and to regulate fishing on the high seas so that all can equally benefit rather than only the few States with adequate fleets. It is important to remember that action at the international level must be guided by the principle of subsidiarity, providing help to individual countries as needed without unnecessarily substituting for their own initiative.

(LS 53–59; L&F 41, 75, 128)

331. What is the best long-term strategy against hunger?

We must remain vigilant about the "hunger problem," consulting many indicators such as local availability of food, prices at the local and global levels, diseases and natural disasters that can affect the particular production of a region or crop, changes in customer tastes or needs, and misconduct on the part of some market participants, especially with regard to speculation. We must also anticipate and react to any concerning decline in the environmental factors that affect food production, such as biodiversity, soil fertility, water reserves, climatic conditions, and the stock of fish in the oceans. At the same time, vigilance over these indicators will only bear fruit if we also address the "great cultural, spiritual and educational challenge [that] stands before us" (LS 202). This is the best long-term strategy.

(LS 202–221; L&F 121, 124–127)

332. What can individual Christians do to fight hunger?

On a personal level, one must take care not to waste food, and to buy food as often as possible that is produced while respecting the environment and allowing workers fair wages and due respect. The recognition that food is not only the fruit of human work, but also a gift of divine providence will help us to be more careful to avoid waste. More broadly, Christians can find in their faith and in their spirituality "ample motivation to care for nature and for the most vulnerable of their brothers and sisters" (LS 64).

On a societal level, the various organizations of civil society and individuals must monitor the actions of their governmental authorities, so that laws and policies truly serve the common good. For example, authorities must avoid exchange agreements that worsen the situation of poor agricultural countries, and they should not promote food as biofuel if this affects food security.

(LS 63–64; L&F 66–68, 85–91)

333. What does the Church do about hunger?

The Church has always manifested a particular concern for the poor, the hungry, and for producers of food. Dioceses, religious orders, and associations like the Caritas network are at the forefront in the fight against hunger and the development of rural communities through training, legal assistance, and the supply of materials and credit. At the international level, the Holy See and the popes have repeatedly urged and continue to charge member States to strive to responsibly resolve the scourge of hunger. They have denounced with particular insistence the "paradox of plenty," referring to those countries with abundant natural resources that suffer incredible poverty. They have also condemned food waste and the use of food as a weapon against innocent people. Furthermore, various Catholic associations conduct dialogues with the private sector, encouraging them to continually improve their performance in ecological, fiscal, and social terms.

(L&F 146–150)

11 The Promotion of Just Peace

MARTIN SCHLAG

Nothing is lost with peace, everything may be lost with war.

POPE PIUS XII, *DECENNIUM DUM EXPLETUR*

Peace goes beyond the mere absence of war; it is fullness of life. It is the goal of every society and is essential to its functioning and flourishing. Peace is constantly threatened by political tensions, war, and terrorism. The Church calls us to forgiveness and moves us to work for peace on the individual, societal, and international levels.

334. What is peace?

Peace is the fruit of justice and love. Peace is a great good and a universal duty founded on an ordering of society that has its roots in God Himself, and is based on justice and charity. Peace is not merely the absence of war, nor can it be reduced solely to maintaining a balance of power between enemies. Violence that is unjust force is never a means to achieving peace.

(CSDC 494–496)

335. What does the Bible teach about peace?

The Bible teaches us that where there is violence, God cannot be present (cf. 1 Chr 22:8–9). Peace is first and foremost a gift from God, one of the greatest gifts God offers to mankind, and it involves obedience to the divine plan. God has established peace as the goal of life in society.

(CSDC 488–490)

336. Is peace part of Christian teaching?

The promise of peace that runs through the entire Old Testament finds its fulfillment in the person of Jesus. Jesus "is our peace" (Eph 2:14). He has broken down the dividing wall of hostility among people, reconciling them with God (cf. Eph 2:14–16). Jesus gives a peace that the world cannot give (cf. Jn 14:27).

(CSDC 491–493)

337. What does the Church teach on war in general? Can war ever be just?

A war of aggression is intrinsically immoral. In the tragic case where such a war breaks out, leaders of the attacked State have the right and the duty to organize a defense using the force of arms. Even in the case of a just defense, however, war is "'the failure of all true humanism,'[1] 'it is always a defeat for humanity'"[2] (CSDC 497). It is therefore better not to speak of a "just war" but of the just defense of peace.

(CSDC 497–500)

338. Under what conditions could the defense of peace through the use of arms be just?

"To be licit, the use of force must correspond to certain strict conditions: 'the damage inflicted by the aggressor on the nation or community of nations must be lasting, grave and certain; all other means of putting an end to it must have been shown to be impractical or ineffective; there must be serious prospects of success; the use of arms must not produce evils and disorders graver than the evil to be eliminated. The power of modern means of destruction weighs very heavily in evaluating this condition'"[3] (CSDC 500).

(CSDC 500–501; CCC 2309)

339. Is it licit for nations to maintain armed forces?

"The requirements of legitimate defense justify the existence in States of armed forces, the activity of which should be at the service of peace. Those who defend the security and freedom of a country, in such a spirit, make an authentic contribution to peace"[4] (CSDC 502).

(CSDC 502)

340. How should the armed forces treat innocent people?

The reason for the existence of armed forces is the legitimate defense of innocent human beings. Therefore, there is a duty to protect and help innocent victims who are not able to defend themselves from acts of aggression. This principle also implies an obligation to spare civil populations from the effects of war. The rules of international humanitarian law delineate acceptable behavior during war.

(CSDC 502–505)

341. Do nations have a duty toward people under attack in other nations?

"The international community as a whole has the moral obligation to intervene on behalf of those groups whose very survival is threatened or whose basic human rights are seriously violated" (CSDC 506). As members of the human family of nations, States cannot remain indifferent. On the contrary, they have the duty to protect: if all other available means should prove ineffective, it is "legitimate and even obligatory to take concrete measures to disarm the aggressor"[5] (CSDC 506). Obviously, the measures adopted must be carried out in full respect of international law and the fundamental principle of equality among States.

(CSDC 506)

342. What does the Church say about arms of mass destruction?

Arms of mass destruction—whether biological, chemical, or nuclear—have been explicitly condemned by the Magisterium: "Any act of war aimed indiscriminately at the destruction of entire cities or extensive areas along with their population is a crime against God and man himself. It merits unequivocal and unhesitating condemnation" (CSDC 509, quoting GS 80). Furthermore, "it is hardly possible to imagine that in an atomic era, war could be used as an instrument of justice" (CSDC 497, quoting PT 127).

(CSDC 497, 509; GS 80)

343. Are there other practices of warfare besides arms of mass destruction that have been singled out as evil by the Magisterium?

The Church demands the total elimination of anti-personnel landmines and of all other weapons that inflict excessively traumatic injury or that strike indiscriminately. She also demands that the use of children and adolescents as soldiers in armed conflicts be stopped.

(CSDC 510–512)

344. What must a member of the armed forces do if he or she receives unjust orders?

Military personnel should obey just orders. However, "every member of the armed forces is morally obliged to resist orders that call for perpetrating crimes against the law of nations and the universal principles of this law[6]....Such acts cannot be justified by claiming obedience to the orders of superiors" (CSDC 503).

(CSDC 503)

345. What should nations do to avoid the tragedy of war?

Seeking alternative solutions to war is a matter of tremendous urgency. Nearly every conflict of interests has the potential to be solved by means other than war, for example, by negotiations. It is essential, however, to seek the causes underlying conflicts, especially those connected with structural situations of injustice, poverty, and exploitation. It can be therefore be said that "another name for peace is *development*" (CSDC 498, quoting CA 52).

(CSDC 498–499)

346. What other means exist for avoiding war besides negotiations and a long-term plan of development?

War is always the last measure, to be used when all other attempts have failed. Before entering into war, the international community should impose sanctions aimed at correcting the behavior of the government of a country that violates the rules of peaceful and ordered international coexistence or that practices serious forms of oppression toward its population.

(CSDC 507)

347. Does the Church advocate disarmament?

Yes. The Church proposes the goal of "general, balanced and controlled disarmament"[7] (CSDC 508). Each State may possess the means necessary for its legitimate defense; however, any stockpiling or indiscriminate trading in arms beyond this measure cannot be morally justified.

(CSDC 508–511)

348. What is terrorism?

Terrorism is one of the most brutal forms of violence. It aims at intimidating and destabilizing public authority or populations by spreading fear and terror among civilians through the destruction of life or property. It often targets innocent people in places of everyday life, making them chance victims of violence.

(CSDC 513)

349. Can terrorism ever be justified? What about those who kill in the name of God?

Terrorism can never be justified for any reason, especially religious reasons. "It is a profanation and a blasphemy to declare oneself a terrorist in God's name"[8] (CSDC 515). Terrorism is to be condemned in the most absolute terms. States have the right and the duty to defend innocent people from terrorism. Such a defense, however, does not justify means that are contrary to international law and human rights.

(CSDS 514–515)

350. How can terrorism most effectively be avoided?

It is important to discover the causes that can lead to terrorism. "The fight against terrorism presupposes the moral duty to help create those conditions that will prevent it from arising or developing" (CSDC 513). In this context, commitment on the political and educational levels is especially urgent, as the recruitment of terrorists is easier in places where injustices occur and human rights are infringed upon.

(CSDC 513–514)

351. Does the Church contribute to world peace?

"The promotion of peace in the world is an integral part of the Church's mission of continuing Christ's work of redemption on earth. In fact, the Church is, in Christ, a "'sacrament" or sign and instrument of peace in the world and for the world"'[9] (CSDC 516). This means that the Church offers the world a community of forgiveness and reconciliation, without which peace is impossible.

(CSDC 516)

352. Can there be peace without forgiveness?

There can be no peace without justice, and no justice without forgiveness. Certainly, "mutual forgiveness must not eliminate the need for justice and still less does it block the path that leads to truth" (CSDC 518). However, every act of violence leaves behind a heavy burden of pain, which cannot simply be done away with, but can only be accepted when mutual forgiveness is offered and received. This is a long and difficult process, but one that is possible.

(CSDC 517–518)

353. What is the Church's most important contribution to peace?

The Church's most important contribution to peace is the celebration of the Eucharist, which is a limitless wellspring for all authentic Christian community, forgiveness, and commitment to peace. The Church engages the battle for peace through prayer. "Prayer opens the heart not only to a deep relationship with God but also to an encounter with others marked by respect, understanding, esteem and love"[10] (CSDC 519).

(CSDC 519–520)

12 Transforming the Culture

MARTIN SCHLAG

Our faith is not just a weekend obligation, a mystery to be celebrated around the altar on Sunday. It is a pervasive reality to be practiced every day in homes, offices, factories, schools, and businesses across our land.

USCCB, *ECONOMIC JUSTICE FOR ALL*, PREFACE, 25

The New Evangelization calls every Christian to go forth and proclaim the gospel, each according to his or her own vocation. This involves the inculturation of the faith. "A faith that does not affect a person's culture is a faith 'not fully embraced, not entirely thought out, not faithfully lived'"[1] (CFL 59). The gospel has the power to renew cultural and social realities, both taking up the good in them and cleansing their sinful elements.

354. Obviously, the social teaching of the Church needs to be put into practice. What is its main contribution to Christian action?

The Church contributes to the building up of the human community by bringing out the social significance of the gospel. The pastoral activity of the Church in the social sector and the social action of Christians always place the human person at the center, especially the poor and suffering. Through their lives and deeds, Christians should strive to shape their societies. Our faith can renew the culture and society in which we live.

(CSDC 521–523, 527)

355. What is culture?

In reference to individual persons, the word "culture" indicates "everything whereby man develops and perfects his many bodily and spiritual qualities" (GS 53). On a societal level, it refers to the sum of all elements that shape our life in society. There are many different cultures because the elements of culture vary according to time and place. Such elements are typically of a technological, symbolic, and institutional nature. Culture is essential for human life; without it we could not fully develop as human beings. Thus culture also has an ethical and religious component.

(GS 53)

356. Does the Christian faith have anything to do with culture?

Yes. A living faith forms and penetrates culture from the inside. It thus renews and cleanses the mores and behaviors in a society. We call this "inculturation."

(CSDC 523)

357. What is the "New Evangelization"?

The New Evangelization, in broad terms, refers to evangelizing those societies that have never known the gospel, and re-evangelizing those societies that have previously experienced the gospel, but have also seen a secularization of their cultures. The New Evangelization thus calls for the inculturation of the Christian faith in present-day society, which begins with the affirmation of the good that exists in our societies, and then strives to cleanse them of their sinful elements. The social teaching plays an important part in this effort.

(CSDC 523)

358. Whom does the Church entrust with spreading the social doctrine and inculturating the faith?

Every Christian and the entire people of God have a role to play in the Church's mission. As baptized members of the faith, it is our honor and duty to share the gift of faith with others. No person can leave the task of evangelization and inculturation of the faith to others. All Christians are also called to perform pastoral work in the social sector. All Christians are called to become active subjects in discovering the truth, and to bear witness to the truth in word and in deed.

(CSDC 525, 538)

359. But aren't there different functions in the Church?

Yes, there are. It is Christ's will that in the Church there are sacred ministers (also called clergy), and other Christian faithful who are called laity. Furthermore, there is a third group of Christians who consecrate themselves to God in a religious order by professing the evangelical counsels. "In virtue of their rebirth in Christ there exists among all the Christian faithful a true equality with regard to dignity and the activity whereby all cooperate in the building up of the Body of Christ in accord with each one's own condition and function"[2] (CCC 872).

(CCC 872; LG 31–32)

360. What is the main task of the pastors of the Church, such as bishops, priests, catechists, and religious brothers and sisters?

The Church has "the duty of scrutinizing the signs of the times and of interpreting them in the light of the Gospel. Thus, in language intelligible to each generation, she can respond to the perennial questions which men ask about this present life and the life to come, and about the relationship of the one to the other. We must therefore recognize and understand the world in which we live, its explanations, its longings, and its often dramatic characteristics" (GS 4). The first task of the pastors of the Church thus consists in listening to their brothers and sisters with keen interest about the social issues of the day, and in the desire to understand and to share.

(CSDC 533)

361. Is that all?

In addition to the fundamental task of sharing the gospel, pastors must also orient, guide, and teach it in its social dimension to their fellow Christians. Our Christian formation is incomplete without knowledge of the social doctrine of the Church. It should be part of the formation of all Christians, particularly of the lay faithful, whose gift and duty it is to take into account their obligations in civil society.

(CSDC 528–531)

362. How should this work of formation be oriented?

The teaching of the Church's social doctrine should be directed toward making life and work in this world more human and more Christian. It does not consist of words alone but should serve to motivate good actions. For this reason, the best catechesis is the witness of a Christian life. Regarding the social teaching of the Church, the first step in the formation of all lay Christians should be to help them fulfill their everyday activities in the cultural, social, economic, and political spheres, and to develop in them a sense of duty that is at the service of the common good. A next step concerns the special formation of those Christians who have the talent and feel the call to serve the community in roles of leadership.

(CSDC 530–531)

363. What is the calling of the lay faithful?

The calling of the lay faithful is to give witness to Christ and to be contemplatives in the middle of the world, which means seeking God in everything they do. We call this "the secular nature of their Christian discipleship" (CSDC 541). It is their duty to proclaim the gospel in word and in deed in all human activities: in the family; in their professional commitments in the world of work, culture, science, and research; and in the exercise of social, economic, and political responsibilities. All secular realities that form the context of their Christian life are matters the lay faithful can transform by a life of holiness.

(CSDC 541–545)

364. How can the lay faithful bring this about?

Lay Catholics are disciples of Christ. Like the clergy and the religious, God marks them with the very image of His Son Jesus Christ through the sacraments. Because of their common priesthood stemming from baptism, the laity can transform secular realities through their work. "The lay faithful are called to cultivate an authentic lay spirituality by which they are reborn as new men and women, both sanctified and sanctifiers, immersed in the mystery of God and inserted in society" (CSDC 545).

(CSDC 542, 545)

365. Is the mission of the lay Catholic only a question of the sacraments and prayer?

No, the lay faithful must become ever more competent in their professional work, thereby carrying out their social duties and strengthening their moral lives. They must strive to acquire the professional and technical skills necessary for their work as well as to grow in virtue. "There cannot be two parallel lives in their existence: on the one hand, the so-called 'spiritual' life, with its values and demands; and on the other, the so-called 'secular' life, that is, life in a family, at work, in social relationships, in the responsibilities of public life and in culture" (CSDC 546, quoting CFL 59).

(CSDC 546)

366. What is the goal of Christians in working together with others in order to improve society?

The essential aim of Christians with regard to the improvement of society is the promotion of human dignity, both in the lives of individuals and in social institutions and structures. In undertaking this task, the conversion of one's own heart must take priority over the renewal of social institutions and structures because concern for others stems from the transformation of one's own heart.

(CSDC 552)

367. Where does the promotion of human dignity begin?

The family, educational institutions, and the Church teach people how to live in accordance with their dignity. "Promoting human dignity implies above all affirming the inviolability of the right to life, from conception to natural death, the first among all rights and the condition for all other rights of the person"[3] (CSDC 553). Furthermore, respect for human dignity requires respect for the religious dimension of the person, that is, the effective recognition of the right to freedom of conscience and the religious freedom of individuals and institutions. In the present cultural context, there is also a particularly urgent need to defend indissoluble marriage between one man and one woman, and to defend the family.

(CSDC 553)

368. Can ecclesial associations, groups, and movements be useful for the evangelization of society and the inculturation of the faith?

These groups can be very helpful because they bring people together in the name of their Christian vocation and mission, and thus multiply efforts. Exchanging experiences and supporting each other in the Christian life within a particular professional or cultural field can promote the formation of mature Christians.

(CSDC 550)

369. Is the social field an area where Catholics should cooperate with other Christian denominations and with believers in other religions?

The social teaching of the Church is a privileged instrument of dialogue among Christians, with the Jews, our elder brethren in the faith, and with believers in other religions. The social problems of our day are so complex and difficult that they can only be tackled together. Such a cooperation will promote awareness of the brotherhood we share with other Christians, and of the spiritual heritage of all religions that obliges all believers to struggle for peace and development.

(CSDC 534–537)

370. What is the ultimate aim and purpose of the social doctrine of the Church?

The ultimate aim and purpose of the social doctrine of the Church is the eternal salvation of souls. This is inseparable from building a "civilization of love" on earth. Toward this end, the Church proposes "the principles and values that can sustain a society worthy of the human person. Among these principles, solidarity includes all the others in a certain way....Love is the only force (cf. 1 Cor 12:31–14:1) that can lead to personal and social perfection, allowing society to make progress towards the good" (CSDC 580). This implies the discovery that all political decisions and economic exchanges stem from human relationships, and that there is a human dimension to them.

(CSDC 580; CV 36)

Special Topic: *Communications and Social Media*

NORBERTO GONZÁLEZ GAITANO

371. What is the Church's general attitude toward the media?

All means of communication are very important for society, and thus also for Catholic social ethics. Since Vatican Council II (cf. Vatican Council II, *Inter Mirifica*, 1–2), and especially with Pope John Paul II's teachings and the testimony of his attitude towards journalists and communicators, the Church has stressed its positive outlook toward the media. At the same time, she continually calls for discernment, since "the world of mass media also has need of Christ's redemption" (John Paul II, Apostolic Letter *The Rapid Development* 2005, 4).

(CSDC 376; John Paul II, Encyclical Letter *Redemptoris Missio* 37)

372. Can we speak of a media ethics? Who would be responsible for it?

When speaking of media-related ethical issues, the Church considers mainly the *people* who work in the media more than the "instruments" of social communication. It only makes sense to talk about morality where free choice is involved; thus it is not the instruments, but what people do with them that is the primary ethical concern. Consequently, we can speak of the moral duties of various groups: media producers, journalists, scriptwriters, film directors, photographers, editors, etc.; media owners; public authorities; and even users of media. Although people speak about "the media" doing this or that, it is not some blind force of nature beyond human control. Even though the use of the media often has unintended consequences, it is still *people* that choose to use the media for good or for evil.

(CSDC 560–561; EC 1)

373. What are the most relevant principles of media ethics?

To begin, it must be said that the community of persons and the human person are the *end* and the *measure* of communication. Ethical principles and norms relevant in other fields also apply to social communication: "Principles of social ethics like solidarity, subsidiarity, justice and equity, and accountability in the use of public resources and the performance of roles of public trust are always applicable. Communication must always be truthful, since truth is essential to individual liberty and to authentic community among persons" (EC 20). Truth further demands the dissemination of responsible information—media content should not promote xenophobia, discrimination, or nationalism disguised as patriotism.

In situations of conflict, the media should be on the side of the weak—of the victims, not of the powerful: "the decision makers have a serious moral duty to recognize the needs and interests of those who are particularly vulnerable—the poor, the elderly and unborn, children and youth, the oppressed and marginalized, women and minorities, the sick and disabled—as well as families and religious groups" (EC 22). At the same time, this must be done without exploiting the vulnerable for ideological purposes.

(CSDC 414–416; PT 90)

374. What should one keep in mind when using the media?

"The first duty of media users is to be discerning and selective. Parents, families and the Church have precise responsibilities they cannot renounce" (CSDC 562). This responsibility is twofold: to "govern" the media consumption of their children, and to educate their children in virtue so as to foster temperance, develop a critical mind, and promote sound prudential judgments.

Catholics have the duty to be correctly informed about the life of the Church. This requires, on the one hand, that the faithful search for reliable sources, and on the other, that pastors be transparent. The faithful, pastors, and people working in Church communications should be aware that their words and actions are at the service of the whole communion of the Church.

375. Does the Church promote freedom of speech?

Yes. The Church upholds freedom of speech, which is closely related to freedom of religion. If one is deprived of the other, they both become devoid of meaning, merely formal and apparent freedoms. Both freedom of speech and freedom of religion are threatened in today's society, especially by religious extremists and intolerant relativism. In the case of the latter, many people have become subject to what recent popes have called the "tyranny" or "dictatorship" of relativism. Without truth, it is power that governs. The powerful often intimidate and even silence believers through political and economic pressure, manipulation, or even psychological abuse.

(PT 12)

376. Are there limits to freedom of speech?

As has been said for the freedom of religion and conscience, the *just limits* of the exercise of the freedom of speech "must be determined in each social situation with political prudence, according to the requirements of the common good, and ratified by the civil authority through legal norms consistent with the objective moral order" (CSDC 422).

377. Can and should the government intervene intervene in this area of speech?

The Church's teaching on freedom of conscience in relation to the common good can easily be applied to freedom of speech. The government can and should intervene when it is needed for "the effective safeguard of the rights of all citizens and for the peaceful settlement of conflicts of rights, also out of the need for an adequate care of genuine public peace, which comes about when men live together in good order and in true justice, and finally out of the need for a proper guardianship of public morality" (DH 7).

378. What makes social media different from other means of communication?

Social media distinguishes itself from "old" media in that its audience participates more actively in the communication process. Users are also content producers themselves, rather than mere consumers. Social media platforms have opened up an entire world, allowing us to share our lives, knowledge, joys, and sorrows with our brothers and sisters across the globe.

379. What are some of the challenges posed by social media and other new technologies?

Social media and other new technologies pose new challenges to human culture inasmuch as they are shaping personal relations and changing family and social relationships: "Today the modern media, which are an essential part of life for young people in particular, can be both a help and a hindrance to communication in and between families. The media can be a hindrance if they become a way to avoid listening to others, to evade physical contact, to fill up every moment of silence and rest, so that we forget that 'silence is an integral element of communication; in its absence, words rich in content cannot exist.' (Benedict XVI, *Message for the World Communications Day* 2012). The media can help communication when they enable people to share their stories, to stay in contact with distant friends, to thank others or to seek their forgiveness, and to open the door to new encounters. By growing daily in our awareness of the vital importance of encountering others,…we will employ technology wisely, rather than letting ourselves be dominated by it. Here too, parents are the primary educators, but they cannot be left to their own devices. The Christian community is called to help them in teaching children how to live in a media environment in a way consonant with the dignity of the human person and service of the common good" (Francis, *Message for the World Communications Day* 2015).

(LS 47)

Notes

Notes to Preface

1. Paul VI, *Address During the Last General Meeting of the Second Vatican Council,* December 7, 1965 (Vatican City: Libreria Editrice Vaticana, 1965). Text in brackets added by editor. Note: all Vatican documents cited in this book, unless otherwise noted, are available at w2.vatican.va/content/vatican/en.html and can usually be discovered through an Internet search by title.

2. See Vatican Council II, *Gaudium et Spes* (Vatican City: Libreria Editrice Vaticana, 1965), Preface, footnote 1.

3. John Paul II, Apostolic Exhortation, *Ecclesia in America* (Vatican City: Libreria Editrice Vaticana, 1999), 54. Note: numbers at the end of the citations of Vatican documents in this book indicate paragraph numbers unless otherwise noted.

Notes to Chapter 1

1. Here the encyclical quotes Paul VI, "Address for the Day of Development, August 23, 1968," *Acta Apostolicae Sedis* 60 (1968), pp. 626–627. Available in Spanish and Italian at https://w2.vatican.va/content/paul-vi/en/homilies/1968.index.html

Notes to Chapter 3

1. Here the *Compendium* references John Paul II, Encyclical Letter *Evangelium Vitae* (Vatican City: Libreria Editrice Vaticana, 1995), 35; *Catechism of the Catholic Church* (Vatican City: Libreria Editrice Vaticana, 1992), 1721.

2. Here the *Compendium* references Pius XII, "Radio Message, December 24, 1944," 5, *Acta Apostolicae Sedis* 37 (1945), p. 12.

3. Here the *Compendium* references the *Catechism of the Catholic Church,* 1956.

Notes to Chapter 4

1. Here the *Compendium* references John XXIII, Encyclical Letter *Mater et Magistra* (Vatican City: Libreria Editrice Vaticana, 1961), 62–67; Paul VI, Apostolic Letter *Octogesima Adveniens* (Vatican City: Libreria Editrice Vaticana, 1971), 46; *Catechism of the Catholic Church* (Vatican City: Libreria Editrice Vaticana, 1992), 1913.

2. Here the *Compendium* references the *Catechism of the Catholic Church,* 1910.

3. Here the *Compendium* references John Paul II, Encyclical Letter *Centesimus Annus* (Vatican City: Libreria Editrice Vaticana, 1991), 49; John Paul II, Encyclical Letter *Sollicitudo Rei Socialis* (Vatican City: Libreria Editrice Vaticana, 1988), 15.

4. Here the *Compendium* references *Centesimus Annus*, 46.

5. Here the *Compendium* references Vatican Council II, *Gaudium et Spes* (Vatican City: Libreria Editrice Vaticana, 1965), 30–31; *Centesimus Annus*, 47.

6. Here the *Compendium* references the *Catechism of the Catholic Church*, 2467.

7. Here the *Compendium* references *Gaudium et Spes*, 16; *Catechism of the Catholic Church*, 2464–2487.

8. Here the *Compendium* references John XXIII, Encyclical Letter *Pacem in Terris* (Vatican City: Libreria Editrice Vaticana, 1963), 118–125.

9. Here the *Compendium* references *Centesimus Annus*, 42, noting: "This statement is made in the context of economic initiative, but it appears correct to apply it also to other areas of personal activity."

10. Here the *Compendium* references John Paul II, Encyclical Letter *Laborem Exercens* (Vatican City: Libreria Editrice Vaticana, 1981), 2.

11. Here the *Compendium* references *Sollicitudo Rei Socialis*, 40; *Catechism of the Catholic Church*, 1929.

12. Here the *Compendium* references John Paul II, *Message for the World Day of Peace*, January 1, 2004 (Vatican City: Libreria Editrice Vaticana, 2004), 10.

13. Here the encyclical quotes Paul VI, "Address for the Day of Development, August 23, 1968," *Acta Apostolicae Sedis* 60 (1968), pp. 626–627. Available in Spanish and Italian at https://w2.vatican.va/content/paul-vi/en/homilies/1968.index.html

14. Here the *Compendium* quotes John Paul II, *Message for the World Day of Peace*, January 1, 2004, 10.

Notes to Chapter 5

1. Here the *Compendium* references Vatican Council II, Decree *Apostolicam Actuositatem* (Vatican City: Libreria Editrice Vaticana, 1965), 11.

Notes to Chapter 6

1. Here the *Catechism* references the *Code of Canon Law* (Vatican City: Libreria Editrice Vaticana, 1983), can. 1248.2.

2. Here the *Compendium* references the *Catechism of the Catholic Church* (Vatican City: Libreria Editrice Vaticana, 1992), 2427; John Paul II, *Laborem Exercens* (Vatican City: Libreria Editrice Vaticana, 1981), 27.

Notes to Special Topics: Immigration

1. Here the *Compendium* references John Paul II, *Message for the World Day of Peace*, January 1, 2001 (Vatican City: Libreria Editrice Vaticana, 2001), 13; Pontifical Council "Cor Unum," *Refugees: A Challenge to Solidarity* (Vatican City: Libreria Editrice Vaticana, 1992), 6.

Notes to Chapter 7

1. Here the encyclical quotes the Paraguayan Bishops' Conference Pastoral Letter *El campesino paraguayo y la tierra*, June 12, 1983 (Asunción, Paraguay: Conferencia Episcopal Paraguaya, 1983), 2.4.d. Available (in Spanish) at http://episcopal. org.py/news-item/el-campesino-paraguayo-y-la-tierra-12-de-junio-de-1983.

Notes to Chapter 8

1. Here the *Compendium* references Encyclical Letter *Pacem in Terris* (Vatican City: Libreria Editrice Vaticana, 1963), 35–38, 75–129, 161–165; John Paul II, Encyclical Letter *Sollicitudo Rei Socialis* (Vatican City: Libreria Editrice Vaticana, 1963), 39.

2. Here the *Compendium* references the *Catechism of the Catholic Church* (Vatican City: Libreria Editrice Vaticana, 1992), 2242.

3. Here the *Compendium* quotes John Paul II, Encyclical Letter *Evangelium Vitae* (Vatican City: Libreria Editrice Vaticana, 1995), 27.

4. Here the *Compendium* references Vatican Council II, Declaration *Dignitatis Humanae* (Vatican City: Libreria Editrice Vaticana, 1965), 3.

5. Here the *Compendium* references the *Catechism of the Catholic Church*, 2108.

Notes to Chapter 9

1. Here the *Compendium* references John XXIII, Encyclical Letter *Pacem in Terris* (Vatican City: Libreria Editrice Vaticana, 1963), 69–72.

2. Here the *Compendium* references Paul VI, Encyclical Letter *Populorum Progressio* (Vatican City: Libreria Editrice Vaticana, 1967), 51–55 and 77–79.

3. Here the *Compendium* references *Populorum Progressio*, 44.

Notes to Chapter 10

1. Here the encyclical quotes John Paul II, *General Audience*, January 30, 2002 (Vatican City: Libreria Editrice Vaticana, 2002), 6.

2. Here the *Compendium* references John Paul II, *Meeting with Scientists and Representatives of the United Nations University, Hiroshima*, February 25, 1981 (Vatican City: Libreria Editrice Vaticana, 1981), 3.

Notes to Chapter 11

1. Here the *Compendium* quotes John Paul II, *Message for the World Day of Peace*, January 1, 1999, (Vatican City: Libreria Editrice Vaticana, 1999), 11.

2. Here the *Compendium* quotes John Paul II, *Address to the Diplomatic Corps*, January 13, 2003 (Vatican City: Libreria Editrice Vaticana, 2003), 4. Reproduced from *L'Osservatore Romano*, English ed., January 15, 2003, p. 3.

3. Here the *Compendium* references the *Catechism of the Catholic Church* (Vatican City: Libreria Editrice Vaticana, 1992), 2309.

4. Here the *Compendium* references Vatican Council II, *Gaudium et Spes* (Vatican City: Libreria Editrice Vaticana, 1965), 79; *Catechism of the Catholic Church*, 2310.

5. Here the *Compendium* references John Paul II, *Message for the World Day of Peace*, January 1, 2000, (Vatican City: Libreria Editrice Vaticana, 2000), 11.

6. Here the *Compendium* references the *Catechism of the Catholic Church*, 2313.

7. Here the *Compendium* references John Paul II, *Message for the Fortieth Anniversary of the United Nations*, October 14, 1985 (Vatican City: Libreria Editrice Vaticana, 1985), 6. Reproduced from *L'Osservatore Romano*, English ed., November 14, 1985, p. 4.

8. Here the *Compendium* references John Paul II, *Address to Representatives from the World of Culture, Art and Science, Astana, Kazakhstan*, September 24, 2001 (Vatican City: Libreria Editrice Vaticana, 2001), 5. Reproduced from *L'Osservatore Romano*, English ed., September 26, 2001, p. 7.

9. Here the *Compendium* quotes John Paul II, *Message for the World Day of Peace*, January 1, 2000, 20.

10. Here the *Compendium* references John Paul II, *Message for the World Day of Peace*, January 1, 1992 (Vatican City: Libreria Editrice Vaticana, 1992), 4.

Notes to Chapter 12

1. Here the apostolic exhortation quotes John Paul II, *Address to the Participants in the National Congress of Church Movements of Cultural Responsibility*, January 16, 1982 (Vatican City: Libreria Editrice Vaticana, 1982), 2. See *Insegnamenti di Giovanni Paolo II*, vol. 5, part 1 (Vatican City: Libreria Editrice Vaticana, 1982), p. 131.

2. Here the *Catechism* references the *Code of Canon Law* (Vatican City: Libreria Editrice Vaticana, 1983), can. 208; cf. Vatican Council II, Dogmatic Constitution *Lumen Gentium* (Vatican City: Libreria Editrice Vaticana, 1964), 32.

3. Here the *Compendium* references the Congregation for the Doctrine of the Faith, "Instruction *Donum Vitae*," *Acta Apostolicae Sedis* 80 (1988), pp. 70–102.

Bibliography

The sources in this bibliography marked with (*) are available online in English at the Vatican website www.vatican.va. Documents of the Congregation for the Doctrine of the Faith may be found through http://www.vatican.va/roman_curia/congregations/cfaith/index.htm

Aquinas, Thomas. *Summa Theologiae*. Cambridge: Blackfriars, 1964.

Benedict XVI. *Christmas Address to the Roman Curia*. December 22, 2005. Vatican City: Libreria Editrice Vaticana.*

————. *Deus Caritas Est*. Encyclical Letter. Vatican City: Libreria Editrice Vaticana, 2005.*

————. *Christmas Address to the Roman Curia*. December 22, 2008. Vatican City: Libreria Editrice Vaticana, 2008.*

————. *Caritas in Veritate*. Encyclical Letter. Vatican City: Libreria Editrice Vaticana, 2009.*

————. *Message for the Celebration of the World Day of Peace: If You Want to Cultivate Peace, Protect Creation*. January 1, 2010. Vatican City: Libreria Editrice Vaticana, 2009.*

————. *Message for the Celebration of the World Day of Peace: Religious Freedom, The Path to Peace*. January 1, 2011. Vatican City: Libreria Editrice Vaticana, 2010.*

————. *Africae Munus*. Apostolic Exhortation. Vatican City: Libreria Editrice Vaticana, 2011.*

————. *Message for the 46th World Communications Day: Silence and Word: The Path of Evangelization*. May 20, 2012. Vatican City: Libreria Editrice Vaticana, 2012.*

Catechism of the Catholic Church. Vatican City: Libreria Editrice Vaticana, 1992.*

Code of Canon Law. Vatican City: Libreria Editrice Vaticana, 1983.*

Compendium of the Catechism of the Catholic Church. Vatican City: Libreria Editrice Vaticana, 2005.*

Congregation for Catholic Education. *Educational Guidance in Human Love*. Vatican City: Libreria Editrice Vaticana, 1983.*

————. *The Religious Dimension of Education in a Catholic School: Guidelines for Reflection and Renewal*. Vatican City: Libreria Editrice Vaticana, 1988.*

Congregation for the Doctrine of the Faith. "Declaration on Procured Abortion." *Acta Apostolicae Sedis* 66 (1974): pp. 730-747.*

————. "Declaration on Euthanasia *Iura et Bona*." *Acta Apostolicae Sedis* 72, 1 (1980): pp. 542-552.*

————. "Instruction *Libertatis Conscientia*." *Acta Apostolicae Sedis* 79 (1987): pp. 554-599.*

————. "Instruction *Donum Vitae*." *Acta Apostolicae Sedis* 80 (1988): pp. 70-102.*

———. "Instruction *Donum Veritatis.*" *Acta Apostolicae Sedis* 82 (1990): pp. 1550-1570.*

———. "Letter to the Bishops of the Catholic Church on the Collaboration of Men and Women in the Church and in the World." *Acta Apostolicae Sedis* 96 (2004): pp. 671-687.*

———. "Instruction *Dignitas Personae.*" *Acta Apostolicae Sedis* 100 (2008): pp. 858-887.*

———. *Doctrinal Note on Some Questions Regarding the Participation of Catholics in Political Life.* Vatican City: Libreria Editrice Vaticana, 2002.*

Francis. *Address to the Students of the Jesuit Schools of Italy and Albania.* June 7, 2013. Vatican City: Libreria Editrice Vaticana, 2013.*

———. *Evangelii Gaudium.* Apostolic Exhortation. Vatican City: Libreria Editrice Vaticana, 2013.*

———. *Lumen Fidei.* Encyclical Letter. Vatican City: Libreria Editrice Vaticana, 2013.*

———. *Morning Meditation.* September 16, 2013. Vatican City: Libreria Editrice Vaticana, 2013.*

———. *Message to the General Assembly of the Pontifical Academy for Life.* February 19, 2014. Vatican City: Libreria Editrice Vaticana, 2014.*

———. *General Audience.* April 15, 2015. Vatican City: Libreria Editrice Vaticana, 2015.*

———. *In-flight Press Conference from the Philippines to Rome.* January 19, 2015. Vatican City: Libreria Editrice Vaticana, 2015.*

———. *Laudato Si'.* Encyclical Letter. Vatican City: Libreria Editrice Vaticana, 2015.*

———. *Meeting with Families in Manila.* January 16, 2015. Vatican City: Libreria Editrice Vaticana, 2015.*

———. *Message for the 49th Annual World Communications Day: Communicating the Family:*
A Privileged Place of Encounter with the Gift of Love. January 23, 2015. Vatican City: Libreria Editrice Vaticana, 2015.*

———. Bull *Misericordiae Vultus.* Vatican City: Libreria Editrice Vaticana, 2015.*

———. *Amoris Laetitia.* Apostolic Exhortation. Vatican City: Libreria Editrice Vaticana, 2016*

John Paul II. *Address in Puebla, Mexico to the Third General Conference of the Latin American Episcopate.* January 28, 1979. Vatican City: Libreria Editrice Vaticana, 1979.*

———. *Familiaris Consortio.* Apostolic Exhortation. Vatican City: Libreria Editrice Vaticana, 1981.*

———. *General Audience.* May 13, 1981. Vatican City: Libreria Editrice Vaticana, 1981. This address is available in Italian, Portuguese, and Spanish via https://w2.vatican.va/content/john-paul-ii/en/audiences/1981.index.html.

———. *Laborem Exercens.* Encyclical Letter. Vatican City: Libreria Editrice Vaticana, 1981.*

———. "Meeting with Scientists and Representatives of the United Nations University, Hiroshima, February 25, 1981." *L'Osservatore Romano* (English ed.), February 26, 1981.*

———. "Address to the Participants in the National Congress of Church Movements of Cultural Responsibility January 16, 1982." *Insegnamenti di Giovanni Paolo II*, vol. 5, part 1. Vatican City: Libreria Editrice Vaticana, 1982.

———. "Message for the Fortieth Anniversary of the United Nations, October 14, 1985." *L'Osservatore Romano* (English ed.), November 14, 1985.*

———. *Sollicitudo Rei Socialis*. Encyclical Letter. Vatican City: Libreria Editrice Vaticana, 1987.*

———. *Christifideles Laici*. Apostolic Exhortation. Vatican City: Libreria Editrice Vaticana, 1988.*

———. *Redemptoris Missio*. Encyclical Letter. Vatican City: Libreria Editrice Vaticana, 1990.*

———. *Centesimus Annus*. Encyclical Letter. Vatican City: Libreria Editrice Vaticana, 1991.*

———. *Message for the 25th Annual World Day of Peace: Believers United in Building Peace*. January 1, 1992. Vatican City: Libreria Editrice Vaticana, 1992.*

———. Letter to Families *Gratissimam Sane*. Vatican City: Libreria Editrice Vaticana, 1994.*

———. *Evangelium Vitae*. Encyclical Letter. Vatican City: Libreria Editrice Vaticana, 1995.*

———. *Letter to Women*. Vatican City: Libreria Editrice Vaticana, 1995.*

———. *Angelus Address in Berlin*. June 23, 1996. Vatican City: Libreria Editrice Vaticana, 1996. This address is available in German, Italian, and Spanish via https://w2.vatican.va/content/john-paul-ii/en/travels/1996/travels/documents/trav_germany-1996.html.

———. *Ecclesia in America*. Apostolic Exhortation. Vatican City: Libreria Editrice Vaticana, 1999.*

———. *Letter to the Elderly*. Vatican City: Libreria Editrice Vaticana, 1999.*

———. *Message for the Celebration of the World Day of Peace: Respect for Human Rights: The Secret of True Peace*. January 1, 1999. Vatican City: Libreria Editrice Vaticana, 1999.*

———. *Address to the 18th International Congress of the Transplantation Society*. August 29, 2000. Vatican City: Libreria Editrice Vaticana, 2000.*

———. *Message for the Celebration of the World Day of Peace: "Peace on Earth to Those Whom the Lord Loves."* January 1, 2000. Vatican City: Libreria Editrice Vaticana, 2000.*

———. "Address to Representatives from the World of Culture, Art and Science, Astana, Kazakhstan, September 24, 2001." *L'Osservatore Romano* (English ed.), September 26, 2001.*

———. *Message for the Celebration of the World Day of Peace: Dialogue Between Cultures for a Civilization of Love and Peace*. January 1, 2001. Vatican City: Libreria Editrice Vaticana, 2001.*

———. *General Audience*. January 30, 2002. Vatican City: Libreria Editrice Vaticana, 2002.

———. *Letter to the President of the Second World Assembly on Ageing.* Vatican City: Libreria Editrice Vaticana, 2002.*

———. *Address to the Diplomatic Corps,* January 13, 2003. Vatican City: Libreria Editrice Vaticana, 2003.*

———. *Message for the Celebration of the World Day of Peace: An Ever Timely Commitment: Teaching Peace.* January 1, 2004. Vatican City: Libreria Editrice Vaticana, 2004.*

———. *The Rapid Development.* Apostolic Letter. Vatican City: Libreria Editrice Vaticana, 2005.*

John XXIII. *Mater et Magistra.* Encyclical Letter. Vatican City: Libreria Editrice Vaticana, 1961.*

———. *Pacem in Terris.* Encyclical Letter. Vatican City: Libreria Editrice Vaticana, 1963.*

New American Bible. Revised Edition. United States Conference of Catholic Bishops, 2011.

Paraguayan Bishops' Conference. Pastoral Letter *El campesino paraguayo y la tierra.* June 12, 1983. Asunción, Paraguay: Conferencia Episcopal Paraguaya, 1983. http://episcopal.org.py/news-item/el-campesino-paraguayo-y-la-tierra-12-de-junio-de-1983.

Paul VI. *Address During the Last General Meeting of the Second Vatican Council, December 7, 1965.* Vatican City: Libreria Editrice Vaticana, 1965.*

———. *Populorum Progressio.* Encyclical Letter. Vatican City: Libreria Editrice Vaticana, 1967.*

———. "Address for the Day of Development, August 23, 1968." *Acta Apostolicae Sedis* 60 (1968): pp. 626–627. Available in Spanish and Italian at https://w2.vatican.va/content/paul-vi/en/homilies/1968.index.html

———. *Octogesima Adveniens.* Apostolic Letter. Vatican City: Libreria Editrice Vaticana, 1971.*

Pius XI. *Quadragesimo Anno.* Encyclical Letter. Vatican City: Libreria Editrice Vaticana, 1931.*

Pius XII. "Radio Message, December 24, 1944." *Acta Apostolicae Sedis* 37 (1945): pp. 10-20.

———. "Apostolic Letter *Decennium Dum Expletur.*" *Acta Apostolicae Sedis* 41 (1949): pp. 450-453.

Pontifical Academy for Life. *Declaration on the Production and the Scientific and Therapeutic Use of Human Embryonic Stem Cells.* Vatican City: Libreria Editrice Vaticana, 2000.*

Pontifical Council "Cor Unum." *Refugees: A Challenge to Solidarity.* Vatican City: Libreria Editrice Vaticana, 1992.*

Pontifical Council for Justice and Peace. *Compendium of the Social Doctrine of the Church.* Vatican City: Libreria Editrice Vaticana, 2004.*

———. *The Vocation of the Business Leader.* Vatican City: Pontifical Council for Justice and Peace, 2012.

———. *Land and Food.* Vatican City: Libreria Editrice Vaticana, 2015.*

Pontifical Council for Social Communications. *Ethics in Communications.* Vatican City: Libreria Editrice Vaticana, 2000.*

Schönborn, Christoph, ed. *Youcat.* San Francisco: Ignatius Press, 2011.

United States Conference of Catholic Bishops. *Economic Justice for All: Pastoral Letter on Catholic Social Teaching and the U.S. Economy.* Washington, D.C.: United States Conference of Catholic Bishops, 1997.

———. *Q&A Regarding the Holy See's Responses on Nutrition and Hydration for Patients in a "Vegetative State."* Washington, D.C.: United States Conference of Catholic Bishops, 2007.

———. *Catholic Social Teaching on Immigration and the Movement of Peoples.* Washington, D.C.: United States Conference of Catholic Bishops. http://www.usccb.org/issues-and-action/human-life-and-dignity/immigration/catholic-teaching-on-immigration-and-the-movement-of-peoples.cfm. Accessed on May 1, 2016.

———. *Frequently Asked Questions About Comprehensive Immigration Reform.* Washington, D.C.: United States Conference of Catholic Bishops. http://www.usccb.org/issues-and-action/human-life-and-dignity/immigration/frequently-asked-questions-comprehensive-immigration-reform.cfm. Accessed on May 1, 2016.

Vatican Council II. *Inter Mirifica.* Decree. Vatican City: Libreria Editrice Vaticana, 1964.*

———. *Lumen Gentium.* Dogmatic Constitution. Vatican City: Libreria Editrice Vaticana, 1964.*

———. *Dignitatis Humanae.* Declaration. Vatican City: Libreria Editrice Vaticana, 1965.*

———. *Gaudium et Spes.* Vatican City: Libreria Editrice Vaticana, 1965.*

———. *Apostolicam Actuositatem.* Decree. Vatican City: Libreria Editrice Vaticana, 1966.*

Contributors

Pau Agulles is Professor of moral theology at the Pontifical University of the Holy Cross, Rome.

Arturo Bellocq is Professor of moral theology at the Pontifical University of the Holy Cross, Rome.

Norberto González Gaitano is Professor of Public Opinion and Communications at the Pontifical University of the Holy Cross, Rome.

Gregorio Guitián is Professor of Theology at the University of Navarre, Pamplona, Spain.

Antonio Malo is Professor of Philosophy at the Pontifical University of the Holy Cross, Rome.

Jennifer E. Miller is Professor of moral theology at Notre Dame Seminary (LA).

Elizabeth Reichert is a research assistant at the Markets, Culture & Ethics Research Centre at the Pontifical University of the Holy Cross, Rome.

Martin Schlag is Professor of moral theology at the Pontifical University of the Holy Cross, Rome, and co-founder of the Markets, Culture and Ethics Center.

Tebaldo Vinciguerra works in the Dicastery for Promoting Integral Human Development (formerly the Secretariat of the Pontifical Council for Justice and Peace).

Index